**Harvard
Business
Review**

on

THRIVING IN EMERGING MARKETS

The Harvard Business Review
Paperback series

If you need the best practices and ideas for the business challenges you face—but don't have time to find them—**_Harvard Business Review_ paperbacks** are for you. Each book is a collection of HBR's inspiring and useful perspectives on a given management topic, all in one place.

The titles include:

Harvard Business Review on Advancing Your Career

Harvard Business Review on Aligning Technology with Strategy

Harvard Business Review on Building Better Teams

Harvard Business Review on Collaborating Effectively

Harvard Business Review on Communicating Effectively

Harvard Business Review on Finding & Keeping the Best People

Harvard Business Review on Fixing Health Care from Inside & Out

Harvard Business Review on Greening Your Business Profitably

Harvard Business Review on Increasing Customer Loyalty

Harvard Business Review on Inspiring & Executing Innovation

Harvard Business Review on Making Smart Decisions

Harvard Business Review on Managing Supply Chains

Harvard Business Review on Rebuilding Your Business Model

Harvard Business Review on Reinventing Your Marketing

Harvard Business Review on Succeeding as an Entrepreneur

Harvard Business Review on Thriving in Emerging Markets

Harvard Business Review on Winning Negotiations

Harvard Business Review

on

THRIVING IN EMERGING MARKETS

Harvard Business Review Press

Boston, Massachusetts

Library of Congress Cataloging-in-Publication Data
Harvard business review on thriving in emerging markets.
     p. cm. — (The Harvard business review paperback series)
   ISBN 978-1-4221-6263-7 (alk. paper)
   1. Developing countries—Commerce.   2. International business enterprises—Developing countries.   3. International trade.   I. Harvard business review.
   HF1413.H3533   2011
   658'.049091724—dc22

                                                      2011007231

Contents

**Harvard
Business
Review**

on

THRIVING IN EMERGING MARKETS

New Business Models In Emerging Markets

Targeting the middle market can be lucrative—but companies won't be able to deliver unless they start from scratch
by Matthew J. Eyring, Mark W. Johnson, and Hari Nair

RIGHT NOW MORE THAN 20,000 multinationals are operating in emerging economies. According to the *Economist,* Western multinationals expect to find 70% of their future growth there—40% of it in China and India alone. But if the opportunity is huge, so are the obstacles to seizing it. On its 2010 Ease of Doing Business Index, the World Bank ranked China 89th, Brazil 129th, and India 133rd out of 183 countries. Summarizing the bank's conclusions, the *Economist* wrote, "The only way that companies can prosper in these markets is to cut costs relentlessly and accept profit margins close to zero."

Yes, the challenges are significant. But we couldn't disagree more with that opinion. We have seen the opportunities of the future on a street corner in Bangalore, in a small city in central India, in a village in Kenya—and they don't require companies to forgo profits. On the surface, nothing could be more prosaic: a laundry, a compact fridge, a money-transfer service. But look closely at the businesses behind these offerings and you will find the frontiers of business model innovation. These novel ventures reveal a way to help companies escape stagnant demand at home, create new and profitable revenue streams, and find competitive advantage.

That may sound overly optimistic, given the difficulty Western companies have had entering emerging markets to date. But we believe they've struggled not because they can't create viable offerings but because they get their business models wrong. Many multinationals simply import their domestic models into emerging markets. They may tinker at the edges, lowering prices—perhaps by selling smaller sizes or by using lower-cost labor, materials, or other resources. Sometimes they even design and manufacture their products locally and hire local country managers. But their fundamental profit formulas and operating models remain unchanged, consigning these companies to selling largely in the highest income tiers, which in most emerging markets aren't big enough to generate sufficient returns.

What's often missing from even the savviest of these efforts is a systematic process for reconceiving the busi-

Idea in Brief

Many Western multinationals expect to find most of their future growth in emerging economies. But they have frequently struggled to exploit the opportunity, relentlessly cutting costs and accepting profit margins close to zero. The problem, say the authors, who are all with the innovation consultancy Innosight, is not that these companies can't create viable offerings but that simply transplanting their domestic business models to the new markets won't work. They must devise fundamentally new models—by identifying an important unmet job consumers need to do; performing that job profitably at a price the customer will pay; and carefully implementing and evolving the model by constantly testing assumptions and making adjustments. Drawing on their experience investing in, incubating, and consulting for companies that have created 20 new business models in developing markets, the authors describe the vast potential demand represented by the "middle market" in emerging economies—the millions of people who have the desire and wherewithal to pay for goods and services, from refrigeration to clothes washing to money transfers, that will help them do the "jobs" no current offering adequately can.

ness model. For more than a decade, through research and our work in both mature and emerging markets, we have been developing our business model innovation and implementation process (see "Reinventing Your Business Model," HBR December 2008, and "Beating the Odds When You Launch a New Venture," HBR May 2010). At its most basic level, the process consists of three steps: *Identify an important unmet job* a target customer needs done; *blueprint a model* that can accomplish that job profitably for a price the customer is willing to pay; and carefully *implement and evolve the model* by testing essential assumptions and adjusting as you learn.

Start in the Middle

Established companies entering emerging markets should take a page from the strategy of start-ups, for which all markets are new: Instead of looking for additional outlets for existing offerings, they should identify unmet needs— "the jobs to be done" in our terminology—that can be fulfilled at a profit. Emerging markets teem with such jobs. Even the basic needs of their large populations may not yet have been met. In fact, the challenge lies less in finding jobs than in settling on the ones most appropriate for your company to tackle.

Many companies have already been lured by the promise of profits from selling low-end products and services in high volume to the very poor in emerging markets. And high-end products and services are widely available in these markets for the very few who can afford them: You can buy a Mercedes or a washing machine, or stay at a nice hotel, almost anywhere in the world. Our experience suggests a far more promising place to begin: between these two extremes, in the vast middle market. Consumers there are defined not so much by any particular income band as by a common circumstance: Their needs are being met very poorly by existing low-end solutions, because they cannot afford even the cheapest of the high-end alternatives. Companies that devise new business models and offerings to better meet those consumers' needs affordably will discover enormous opportunities for growth.

Take, for example, the Indian consumer durables company Godrej & Boyce. Founded in 1897 to sell locks,

Godrej is today a diversified manufacturer of everything from safes to hair dye to refrigerators and washing machines. In workshops we conducted with key managers in the appliances division, refrigerators emerged as a high-potential area: Because of the cost both to buy and to operate them, traditional compressor-driven refrigerators had penetrated only 18% of the market.

The first thing these managers wanted to know, naturally enough, was "Could Godrej provide a cheaper, stripped-down version of our higher-end refrigerator?" We asked them to consider instead the key needs of those with poor or no refrigeration. Did they know what those consumers really wanted? In a word, no. A small team was assigned to conduct detailed observations, open-ended interviews, and video ethnography to illuminate the job to be done for that untapped market.

The semiurban and rural people the team observed typically earned 5,000 to 8,000 rupees (about $125 to $200) a month, lived in single-room dwellings with four or five family members, and changed residences frequently. Unable to afford conventional refrigerators in their own homes, they were making do with communal, usually secondhand ones.

The shared fridges weren't meeting these people's needs very well, but not for the reasons one might expect. The observers found that they almost invariably contained only a few items. Their users tended to shop daily and buy small quantities of vegetables and milk. Electricity was unreliable, putting even the little food they did want to preserve at risk. What's more, although they wanted to cool their drinking water, making ice wasn't a job for which these people would "hire" a refrigerator.

The team concluded that what this group needed to do was to stretch one meal into two by preserving leftovers and to keep drinks cooler than room temperature—a job markedly different from the one higher-end refrigerators do, which is to keep a large supply of perishables on hand, cold or frozen. Clearly, there was no reason to spend a month's salary on a conventional refrigerator and pay steep electricity prices to get the simpler job done. And just as clearly, the solution wasn't a cheaper conventional fridge. Here was an opportunity to create a fundamentally new product for the underserved middle market.

Targeting this market has two great advantages. First, it's easier to upgrade the solution to a job people are already trying to do than to create sufficient customer demand where none yet exists—as would-be vendors of purified water and other seemingly essential offerings have found to their dismay. Second, it's easier to reach people who are already spending money to get their jobs done. That's essentially what Ratan Tata did with the $2,500 Nano. He didn't ask, "How can I get people who've never bought any form of transportation to buy a car?" He asked, "How can I produce a better alternative for people who hire motor scooters to transport their families?" The goal is to redirect existing demand by offering a clear path from an unsatisfactory solution to a better one.

Offer Unique Benefits for Less

To redirect demand, your customer value proposition (CVP) must solve a problem more effectively, simply, accessibly, or affordably than the alternatives. In developing markets, we have found, the components of a CVP that matter most are affordability and access. Let's look at each in turn.

Affordability

Western companies know that they need to come up with lower-cost offerings in emerging markets, but they too often limit themselves to providing less for less. In 2001, for instance, a 300 ml bottle of Coke cost 10 rupees—a day's wages, on average, and a luxury the company estimated only 4% of the population could afford. To reach the other 96%, it introduced a 200 ml bottle and cut the price in half, shaving margins to make Coke more competitive with common alternatives such as lemonade and tea.

In our experience, though, a far more robust approach to creating an affordable emerging market offering is to trade off expensive features and functions that people don't need for less-expensive ones they do need. To get that right requires a clear understanding of the context in which the offering will be sold—which calls for further fieldwork, preferably of a collaborative rather than a merely observational kind. This is good product-development advice in any market. In fact, it applies to indigenous players operating close to home, like Godrej, as well as to Western companies confronting the unfamiliar.

7

Godrej's team designed and built a prototype cooling unit from the ground up and tested it in the field with consumers. Then, in February 2008, more than 600 women in Osmanabad, a city in India's Marathwada region, gathered to participate in a cocreation event. Working with the original prototypes and several others that had followed, they collaborated with Godrej on every aspect of the product's design. They helped plan the interior arrangements, made suggestions for the lid, and provided insights on color (eventually settling on candy red).

The result was the ChotuKool ("little cool"), a top-opening unit that, at 1.5 x 2 feet and with a capacity of 43 liters, has enough room for the few items users want to keep fresh for a day or two. With only 20 (rather than the usual 200) parts, it has no compressor, cooling tubes, or refrigerant. Instead it uses a chip that cools when a current is applied and a fan like those that prevent desktop computers from overheating. Its top-opening design keeps most of the cold air inside when the lid is opened. It uses less than half the energy of a conventional refrigerator and can run on a battery during the power outages that are common in rural villages. At just 7.8 kilograms, it's highly portable, and at $69, it costs half what the most basic refrigerator does. Because it's the right size for the job, easier to move, and more reliable in a power outage than a conventional fridge, it surpasses the higher-end offering on the performance measures that matter most to these consumers.

Access

It's not surprising that portability is important to potential ChotuKool customers, given that they move frequently. And because populations in emerging markets tend to be dispersed, obtaining goods and services can be more difficult than in the West. This creates opportunities for companies that solve challenges of access.

In Kenya, for example, banking services are scarce and transferring money is complicated and expensive. Without access to traditional services, many people must use unsafe alternatives such as *hawala*—an unregulated network of brokers operating on the honor system—or transport cash by bus. The UK-based Vodafone solved this problem by developing a secure, low-cost mobile money-transfer service. Called M-PESA (*M* for "mobile" and *PESA* from the Swahili word for "money"), the system is operated by Safaricom, Kenya's leading mobile network.

Customers register free with an authorized M-PESA agent—typically a Safaricom dealer, but sometimes a gas station, food market, or other local shop. Once registered, they can deposit or withdraw cash at the agent or transfer money electronically to any mobile phone user, even if the recipient is not a Safaricom subscriber. They can also buy Safaricom airtime for themselves or other subscribers. Customers pay a flat fee of about US 40 cents for person-to-person transfers, 33 cents for withdrawals under $33, and 1.3 cents for balance inquiries. Vodafone (which owns a significant stake in Safaricom) manages individual customer accounts on its server, and Safaricom deposits its customers' balances in pooled accounts in two regulated banks, so their full value is backed by highly liquid assets.

Since its launch, in March 2007, the service has acquired more than 9 million customers—40% of Kenya's adult population. As of June 2010, the *Economist* reported, M-PESA customers could conduct transactions at some 17,900 retail outlets, more than half of them in rural areas. That figure dwarfs the total number of bank branches, post offices, and Post Banks—which is only about 840 nationwide.

Spurred by the success of its original offerings, the service has expanded to include bill payment, business-to-customer payments such as paychecks and microfinance loan disbursements, delivery of humanitarian aid, and international money transfers. After just three years M-PESA accounted for 9% of Safaricom's total revenue. More important, it has become the engine driving the company's profits, which have shifted dramatically from voice to data traffic. Vodafone has launched similar services in Tanzania, Afghanistan, and South Africa and plans to introduce them in Egypt, Fiji, and Qatar as well.

Failure to address the access challenge is an important reason that so many companies have little success adapting their current models to emerging markets. Time and again, the increased volume they hope will offset slimmer profit margins doesn't in fact result in profits, because the costs of serving far-flung customers in infrastructure-poor developing countries are just too high. But companies that, like Vodafone, devise novel approaches may find them to be widely applicable in many markets.

Integrate the Elements

Business models can be conceived in a variety of ways. Our approach focuses on the basics and also on factors that make it difficult to move from an existing model to a new one—margin requirements, overhead, and "resource velocity" (the capacity to generate a given volume of business within a specific time frame). It has four parts: the customer value proposition, a profit formula, key processes, and key resources the company must use to deliver the CVP repeatedly and at scale. Creating competitive advantage lies in integrating these elements to produce value for both the customer and the company. That's easy to say but devilishly hard to do. Mapping the traditional functions of your company to these broad categories will show you how much you'd have to change to integrate those functions into a new business model (see the exhibit "Building a new model").

Once you've devised a CVP for your proposed offering, consider the basis on which you compete—differentiation or price. Offerings that compete on differentiation require that you ask, "What do I have to do to produce this?" which leads you counterclockwise around the model, looking first at what resources and processes are needed, the cost of which (both fixed and variable) will determine what price can deliver the desired profit margin. That's what Whole Foods did when it created a new market for organic foods. Costs drove prices.

For offerings that compete on the basis of price, you move clockwise around the model, again starting with the CVP, but next setting the price, devising a rough

Building a new model

Business models must integrate four elements: the customer value proposition (CVP), the profit formula, key processes, and key resources. Developing new business models always begins with devising a new CVP. Models designed to compete on differentiation next establish the resources and processes needed to deliver the CVP, the cost of which determines the price required in the profit formula. Models designed to compete on price proceed in the opposite way, establishing first the offering's price, then the cost structure, and finally the processes and resources required.

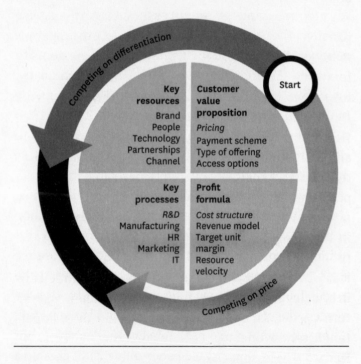

cost structure, and then determining what processes and resources (often radically different from those in your current model) are needed to meet your price requirements. Because affordability is so critical in emerging markets, the decision journey is almost invariably clockwise. Innovators start with a revenue model—"We think we can sell this offering to X number of people at price Y"—and then devise the cost structure required to deliver a certain unit margin. Becoming profitable at that margin means operating at a certain resource velocity, which in turn drives decisions about how to organize operations, what materials to use, and other questions.

More often than not, this exercise reveals that a company can't meet its profit goals in emerging markets merely by reducing variable costs in its current profit formula and that a viable model will require changes to fixed costs or overhead as well. That's what Ratan Tata discovered when he set out to produce his $2,500 car. He couldn't just send the car down the production line and somehow spend less to make it. He needed to reduce fixed costs by designing a car with far fewer parts and changing assembly methods and other key processes. Implementing models that require changes in overhead, margins, or resource velocity tends to be problematic for incumbent companies, which is why it's not surprising that start-ups so often have the edge in bringing to market offerings that require new ways to turn a profit. An open mind is perhaps the most important asset anyone can bring to emerging markets. We learned that lesson when we set out to solve a basic but knotty cleaning problem for a vast group of frustrated consumers.

Village Laundry Service—which was founded by our company and uses the Chamak brand—was aimed squarely at the emerging middle market. In India people who can't afford a washing machine but want an alternative to laborious washing by hand after a long day's work have unappealing choices: They can patronize a *dhobi* (a traditional washing person), or they can take their clothes to a neighborhood laundry or dry-cleaning establishment. The dhobis are cheap, but they use any available water, which can be unhygienic. They slap the clothes against rocks to clean them, which wears down the fabrics, and they don't compensate customers for damage. Turnaround time is five to seven days. A laundry or dry cleaner can do the job in four or five days, generally returns the clothes in good shape, and makes amends if something goes wrong. A laundry may or may not use clean water, however, and both are far more expensive than a dhobi.

In early 2009 we ventured into several parts of India, from urban slums to rural villages, conducting interviews and immersing ourselves in the lives of the people who faced this frustrating choice. What, exactly, was the job to be done? What sort of laundry service would these customers hire? We discovered several things: The job wasn't to make it affordable for them to clean their clothes the way rich people did; it was to replicate the advantage of a home washer and dryer at a price they could afford. It wouldn't be sufficient to get the clothes back in four days—they'd have to be ready within 24 hours, and at a price well below the laundry's or dry cleaner's. And they'd have to be easy to pick up at a nearby location.

With those requirements clearly in mind, we examined all parts of the business model to come up with an inventive way of extending access while keeping costs low. We immediately realized that it would be hard to create a profitable business that placed many traditional self-service laundries across a town, because demand was unpredictable and up-front capital investment and rental deposits would be high. Our solution: Portable seven-foot-square kiosks, each holding an efficient front-loading washer and a dryer, which can be placed wherever there is heavy foot traffic. Customers drop off their clothes to be washed, dried, and ironed, all within 24 hours. The kiosk's small footprint minimizes rents, and its independent water supply, delivered through a fixed contract, is both less expensive and more reliable than the public utility connection. Covered with ads for the Chamak brand, the kiosks also serve as billboards, reducing the need for paid advertising. We keep transaction costs low through an innovative point-of-sale system, made up of a cell phone linked to a Bluetooth printer and report server, which prints receipts, tracks orders, and captures data on business volume.

After much experimentation, we developed standard procedures for staffing and running the kiosks, including tests to gauge potential operators' aptitude and commitment; simple picture-based operating instructions (much like those used in fast-food restaurants) to ensure consistent service; and a scorecard for traffic level, customer satisfaction, marketing effectiveness, and other variables, allowing us to predict the chances of success at each location and to make operations replicable and scalable.

It is this innovative marriage of a novel solution with all the other elements of the business model that makes Chamak's services affordable and profitable. The model allows the company to charge 40 rupees (about $1) per kilogram of clothing—little more than what dhobis charge and significantly less than what professional laundries and dry cleaners do (sometimes 90 rupees per garment). Village Laundry Service currently has 5,000 customers patronizing some 20 booths in Mumbai, Bangalore, and Mysore. The company expects to reach breakeven in late 2011. Of course, as with any new business, how Village Laundry Service performs over the long term will depend on a number of hard-to-predict factors.

From Blueprint to Operating Business

Testing and implementing the business model blueprint in emerging markets is as much an art as a science. Having a cadre of global "experts" study the market for months and create a plan that is then handed over to the local team for execution simply doesn't work. Quick adjustments based on early lessons learned on the ground trump the best and most detailed strategic plan developed before the fact.

M-PESA succeeded in part because Kenya's banking regulator permitted Safaricom to test various business models from the very beginning. Safaricom made the most of the opportunity. It started in 2004 by experimenting with 500 customers and a system designed to allow them to repay microloans. As the company market-tested this concept, it discovered a more-compelling

Four ways to uncover unmet needs

1 **Study what your customers are doing with your product.** Be aware that, as Peter Drucker famously said, "The customer rarely buys what the business thinks it sells him."

2 **Look at the alternatives to your offerings that consumers buy.** Investigate a wide range of substitutes for your products, not just what your competitors make.

3 **Watch for compensating behaviors.** Discover what jobs people are satisfying poorly.

4 **Search for explanations.** Uncover the root causes of consumers' behavior by asking what people are trying to accomplish with the goods and services they use.

value proposition—namely, a way for urban workers to transfer funds to friends and family members in rural areas. That fundamental insight was the basis on which subsequent services were built, and since M-PESA's commercial launch, its simple but powerful branding message has been "Send money home."

This doesn't mean that expertise is unimportant when launching a new business in an emerging market. But we've found that agile functional expertise is the most critical kind, because the uncertainties in emerging markets are so great. A broad network of resources— including responsive advertising agencies, companies that can produce prototypes on demand, financial service advisers who understand local regulatory guidelines, and a healthy bench of local entrepreneurs to execute the plan—is essential.

The ability to conduct rapid experiments inexpensively and use what you learn from them to hone the business model is essential to success. It allows you to make course corrections before you commit to major operational or strategic investments. Recently a company we incubated was looking to launch a men's grooming business but was uncertain about demand. Rather than commission an expensive 10-city quantitative research study, we rented a small air-conditioned truck and created a mini hair salon on wheels, outfitted with a barber's chair, scissors and other implements, and a mirror. For two weeks we drove the truck around the streets of Bangalore to gauge demand and test various pricing scenarios at various locations. The experiment, which cost all of $3,000, provided essential answers that no survey could have and demonstrated the business potential for an affordable and convenient Supercuts-like business for men. The company changed from a roving barbershop model to a kiosk-based model and is considering offering additional services, such as facials and skin lightening, that many customers desire.

Ultimately, the potential for such business model innovations, as for many other disruptive innovations, may extend far beyond the markets for which they were created. G. Sunderraman, the vice president of corporate development at Godrej, sees the ChotuKool as a new growth platform. Unit sales are projected to reach 10,000 in the first year and 100,000 by the end of the second. If Godrej considered the ChotuKool to be simply a no-frills refrigerator for the middle market, it might be content with a moderate penetration rate. But the company's managers regard it as a new product category, based on new technology, that has the potential to perform jobs for people at many income levels. In areas with frequent power outages, the owners of conventional refrigerators might want an inexpensive and reliable backup. Small shops, offices, and manufacturing sites might use it to maintain a supply of cool drinks. Higher-income customers—perhaps in developed economies as well—might use it in their bedrooms, their cars, or their boats. When the technology improves, Godrej believes, it can enter mainstream markets as ChotuKool changes consumers' expectations about refrigerator prices and performance and addresses a need that previously went unmet.

––––––––––

Many companies view emerging markets as one large foothold market, and in this they are right. Classic disruptive innovation theory holds that, ideally, innovations should first be introduced in markets where the alternatives fall short on some dimension (typically price) or are utterly unavailable. Emerging markets fit that bill in spades. They are excellent arenas for trying out product innovations far from competitors' prying eyes. But we are convinced that a much greater opportunity lies in viewing these markets not as one vast lab for product R&D but as unique environments filled with poorly done jobs that could be creatively addressed with business model R&D. Creating new business models will give your company a more enduring competitive advantage.

MATTHEW J. EYRING is the president of Innosight, a strategic innovation consulting and investment firm with offices in Boston, Singapore, and India. **MARK W. JOHNSON** is the chairman of Innosight and the author of *Seizing the White Space: Business Model Innovation for Growth and Renewal* (Harvard Business Review Press, 2010). **HARI NAIR** is a venture partner in India at Innosight's business-building arm, Innosight Labs.

Originally published in January 2011. Reprint R1101E

China vs the World

by Thomas M. Hout and Pankaj Ghemawat

IN THE CITY OF SHANGHAI, a few churches conduct daily services for the faithful, just as churches all over the world do. However, China's Patriotic Catholic Association doesn't operate under the auspices of the Roman Catholic Church, which the Chinese government has banned. It is controlled by a state agency, the Religious Affairs Bureau. That's how the Chinese government deals with foreign organizations, be they churches or companies. They are tolerated in China but can operate only under the state's supervision. They can bring in their ideas if they deliver value to the country, but their operations will be circumscribed by China's goals. If the value—or danger—from them is high, the government will create hybrid organizations that it can better control. This approach, which never ceases to shock foreigners, guides those who are boldly fashioning a new China.

At 61, the People's Republic of China displays all the confidence of a nation that has overcome a midlife economic crisis. Nearly unscathed by the worst global recession in recent history, it is poised to reclaim its place as one of the world's preeminent economies. The days of double-digit growth may be over, but the Chinese economy still expanded by 9% a year from 2008 to 2010. In August 2010 China passed Japan to become the second-largest economy in the world, and next year it is projected to become its biggest manufacturer, pushing the U.S. into second place. That will mark the return to the top spot for a nation that, according to economic historians, was the world's leading manufacturer for 1,500 years, until around 1850, when Britain overtook it during the second industrial revolution.

Even as China moves up the ranks of economic superpowers, many discount these recent milestones. They don't believe that China will become richer than the U.S.—in 2010 America's GDP was three times China's, and its per capita GDP was about 10 times greater, at the official exchange rate—or replace the U.S. as the wellspring of new technologies and other innovations any time soon. But almost unnoticed by the outside world, over the past four years China has been moving toward a new stage of development. It is quietly and deliberately shifting from a successful low- and middle-tech manufacturing economy to a sophisticated high-tech one, by cajoling, co-opting, and often coercing Western and Japanese businesses.

The government plans to increase China's R&D expenditures from the current level, 1.7% of GDP, to 2.5% of GDP by 2020; the U.S. figure today is 2.7%. Like Western governments, it is funding megaprojects in sunrise

Idea in Brief

No longer content with being the world's factory for low-value products, China has quietly opened a new front in its campaign to become the globe's most powerful economy: It's on a quest for high-tech dominance. In pursuit of this goal, the Chinese government has ensured that it will be both buyer and seller in certain key industries by retaining ownership of customers and suppliers alike. It has consolidated manufacturers in those industries into a few national champions to generate economies of scale and concentrate learning. And it is co-opting, cajoling, and coercing multinational corporations to part with their latest technologies, imposing regulations that put those companies in a terrible bind: They can either comply with the rules and share their technologies with would-be Chinese competitors or refuse and miss out on the world's fastest-growing market. Foreign companies doing business in China cannot wait for balancing macroeconomic forces or multilateral solutions; if they wish to survive as global technology leaders, they must bring greater imagination to bear on the problem. Above all, China's maneuvers cast into doubt the optimistic premise that engagement and interdependence with the West would cause capitalism and socialism to converge quickly, reducing international tensions. Storm clouds are gathering over China and the U.S. in particular. Can two economies with such radically different structures and objectives peacefully coexist? Most people expect that the systems will eventually become more similar. However, the authors argue, this will happen only when China becomes as rich—and as technologically advanced— as the U.S.

areas such as new-generation nuclear reactors, nanotechnology, quantum physics, clean energy, and water purification. At the same time, the government is forcing multinational companies in several sectors to share their technologies with Chinese state-owned enterprises as a condition of operating in the country. This is fueling tensions between Beijing and foreign governments and companies, and it raises the critical issue of whether the Chinese brand of socialism can coexist with Western capitalism.

Our studies show that since 2006 the Chinese government has been implementing new policies that seek to appropriate technology from foreign multinationals in several technology-based industries, such as air transportation, power generation, high-speed rail, information technology, and now possibly electric automobiles. These rules limit investment by foreign companies as well as their access to China's markets, stipulate a high degree of local content in equipment produced in the country, and force the transfer of proprietary technologies from foreign companies to their joint ventures with China's state-owned enterprises. The new regulations are complex and ever changing. They reverse decades of granting foreign companies increasing access to Chinese markets and put CEOs in a terrible bind: They can either comply with the rules and share their technologies with Chinese competitors—or refuse and miss out on the world's fastest-growing market.

Just as securing natural resources often drives China's foreign policy, shifting the origination of leading technologies to China is driving the country's industrial policy. In late 2009 China's Ministry of Science and Technology demanded that all the technologies used in products sold to the government be developed in China, which would have forced multinational companies to locate many more of their R&D activities in a country where intellectual property is notoriously unsafe. After howls of protest from foreign governments and companies, the ministry backed down. However, the government still appears intent on creating a tipping point at which multinational companies will have to locate their most-sophisticated R&D projects and facilities in China, enabling it to eventually catch up with or supplant the U.S. as the world's most-advanced economy.

This strategy, which we will describe in the following pages, has provoked several disputes between the Chinese government and foreign companies and caused some companies to review their strategies, along one of two lines. The first seeks to tackle the issue of how a multinational company can minimize competitive and security risks to its technologies. The second approaches the issue from the opposite direction, asking which innovations a foreign company must develop in China in order to gain advantage in the fast-changing global marketplace.

Above all, China's strategy casts into doubt the optimistic premise that engagement and interdependence with the West would cause capitalism and socialism to converge quickly, reducing international tensions. Unsurprisingly, during the recession storm clouds have gathered over U.S.–Chinese relations. The U.S. considers China a currency manipulator and believes it has failed to meet all its commitments to the World Trade Organization, prompting worries about a coming trade war between the two great economic powers of the 21st century. This isn't just a fight over the rules of globalization; it's a larger issue about the inherent difficulties of connecting two big, very different economic systems. Textbook theory suggests that imbalances trigger adjustments, but when economies are very different structurally and follow rigid policies, yoking them together will generate more imbalances—not equilibrium—and heighten tensions. CEOs eager to add another chapter to their lucrative China stories would do well to remember that the relationship between China and the West is historically unstable and to be prepared for unexpected twists and turns.

The Drivers of China's Discontent

China's determination to become a technologically advanced economy is driven as much by economic disillusionment with serving as the world's factory for low-value products as it is by pragmatism.

Disenchantment has set in because in spite of China's huge trade surpluses with the U.S. and Western Europe, the greatest profits have been reaped by foreign rather than Chinese companies, except for a handful of state-owned behemoths. Foreign companies dominate most of China's high-tech industries, accounting for 85% of the high-tech exports from China in 2008. In value terms the picture is no different: Exports of cellular telephones and laptops, for instance, had less than 10% Chinese content—and foreign-owned factories accounted for most of it. The rest of the hardware and software was imported. Frustrated by the inability of Chinese companies to get a larger share of these markets and forced to pay foreign companies ever-larger royalties as demand grows, Beijing decided four years ago to dramatically increase the number of created-in-China technologies.

The government also realized that the renminbi's inevitable appreciation would eventually render China's low-tech exports uncompetitive, and that their manufacture would shift to countries such as Indonesia, Malaysia, Thailand, and Vietnam. To keep its economy growing at around 9%, provide jobs for the next generation of better-educated workers, and boost income levels, the state had to ensure that Chinese companies develop, manufacture, and export advanced products. However, Chinese enterprises, such as the aircraft manufacturer Aviation Industry Corporation of China (AVIC), the wind energy companies Sinovel and Goldwind, and the rail-transport-equipment companies CSR and CNR, were unable to compete technologically with Western, Japanese, and South Korean market leaders.

The Chinese government therefore developed a three-pronged plan to contain foreign companies and enable its companies to create advanced technologies. One, the state has ensured that it will be both buyer and seller in certain key industries, by retaining ownership of customers and suppliers alike. For instance, the Chinese government owns CSR and China Railways, AVIC and China Eastern Airlines. This gives the state a great deal of influence over equipment purchases, sales, and technology development. Two, the government has consolidated several manufacturers into a few national champions, to generate economies of scale and concentrate learning. CSR and AVIC both resulted from the mergers of several smaller, loss-making enterprises.

Three, Chinese officials have learned to tackle multi-national companies, often forcing them to form joint ventures with its national champions and transfer the latest technology in exchange for current and future business opportunities. Companies that resist are simply excluded from projects. The Chinese government uses the restrictions to drive wedges between foreign rivals vying to land big projects in the country and

China's growing R&D

Over the past decade, China has hiked its R&D expenditures by about 21% a year. During the same period, U.S. R&D spending grew by less than 4% a year. If these growth rates continue, China's R&D spending will catch up with that of the U.S. by 2020. Factor in the belief that the renminbi is undervalued by 40%, and China's R&D spending will match that of the U.S. by 2016.

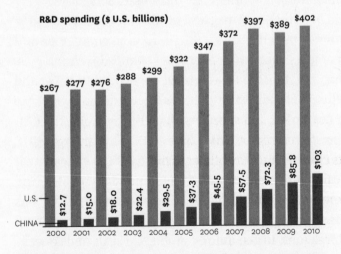

R&D spending ($ U.S. billions)

	2000	2001	2002	2003	2004	2005	2006	2007	2008	2009	2010
U.S.	$267	$277	$276	$288	$299	$322	$347	$372	$397	$389	$402
CHINA	$12.7	$15.0	$18.0	$22.4	$29.5	$37.3	$45.5	$57.5	$72.3	$85.8	$103

Sources: National Science Foundation (U.S.), Ministry of Science and Technology (China).

induce them to transfer the technologies that state-owned enterprises need to catch up. Executives working for multinational companies in China privately acknowledge that making official complaints or filing lawsuits usually does little good.

Timing is critical: The government is convinced that Chinese companies must acquire the latest technologies and invest in R&D immediately if they don't want to miss the local and global infrastructure-building booms now under way. It's also advantageous to act while the renminbi is still undervalued. The government's hope is that the country will soon become a global innovation center matching the U.S. and Western Europe, and that this position will enable Chinese companies to overtake their foreign partners. This logic hinges on the fact that leading-edge technologies usually emerge in countries where the biggest and most-demanding customers are located, and that these customers provide domestic manufacturers with global advantage; think of French manufacturers of nuclear power reactors and American manufacturers of long-haul aircraft. One early indicator supporting this rationale: Applied Materials, a global leader in semiconductor-making equipment, recently transferred many R&D activities to China and relocated its chief technology officer there.

Local-content requirements, mandatory joint ventures, forced technology transfers—these aren't new elements in Asian development strategies. Japan, South Korea, and India, among others, have used them and were less tolerant of foreign investment than China has been. However, the Chinese government is remarkable in how aggressively it applies these policies, how many of its agencies are involved, how quickly and radically it changes the rules, how many unique technology and product standards it tries to impose, and how subtly its regulations violate the spirit, if not the letter, of multilateral agreements. The WTO's broad prohibitions on technology transfers and local-content requirements are more complex and easier to subvert than its rules pertaining to international trade in products. Furthermore, China hasn't yet signed the level-playing-field provisions covering government procurement; it claims that its policies don't violate them, because the WTO allows domestic policy concerns to be accommodated in government purchases. Although the WTO prohibits mandatory technology transfers, the Chinese government maintains that incentivized transfers, whereby companies trade technology for market access, are purely business decisions.

The State's Strategies

The Chinese government has deployed several strategies to help local companies acquire state-of-the-art technologies and break into the global market. Some work in a top-down fashion, others from the bottom up.

Beijing drives the process nationally in most capital-intensive sectors. Consider high-speed railway systems, now an estimated $30 billion a year market in China. In the early 2000s the superior equipment of multinational corporations such as Alstom, which built France's TGV train system; Kawasaki, which helped develop Japan's

China's Plans for Winning the Tech War

FOUR YEARS AGO BEIJING announced its desire to make China an innovation-oriented society.

China wants to strengthen innovation, particularly in energy, transportation, the environment, agriculture, information, and health. It aims to boost the development of proprietary intellectual property. It seeks to apply modern technologies to public life and urbanization. And it is looking to modernize its defense capabilities, including its space program.

Accordingly, Beijing plans to increase R&D spending from 1.5% of GDP in 2006 to 2.5% by 2020, introduce unique technical standards that would reduce dependence on imported technologies by 30%, and ensure that China will become one of the world's top five economies according to the number of patents granted and scientific papers published. The government is using four mechanisms to achieve these goals:

1. It offers tax incentives, including accelerated depreciation of investments in R&D facilities and tax breaks on returns from venture capital investments in technology-based start-ups.

2. It has increased spending in 17 areas in which the state's research institutions and its enterprises collaborate, banks offer cheap loans, and special funding supports the development of domestic technologies that can replace imported ones.

3. It has tailored procurement policies to favor indigenously developed technologies. This occurs at the national, provincial, and municipal levels, especially in cities such as Beijing, Shanghai, and Guangzhou, where the state wants technology-rich industries to replace low- and mid-tech ones that are moving inland.

4. Finally, as described in the main text, it is forcing multinational companies to transfer their newest technologies to their joint ventures with China's state-owned companies.

bullet trains; and Siemens, the German engineering conglomerate, gave foreign companies control of about two-thirds of the Chinese market. The multinationals subcontracted the manufacture of simple components to state-owned companies and delivered end-to-end systems to China's railway operators. In early 2009 the government began requiring foreign companies wanting to bid on high-speed railway projects to form joint ventures with the state-owned equipment producers CSR and CNR. Multinational companies could hold only a 49% equity stake in the new companies, they had to offer their latest designs, and 70% of each system had to be made locally. Most companies had no choice but to go along with these diktats, even though they realized that their joint-venture partners would soon become their rivals outside China.

The multinationals are still importing the most-sophisticated components, such as traction motors and traffic-signaling systems, but today they account for only 15% to 20% of the market. CSR and CNR have acquired many of the core technologies, applied them surprisingly quickly, and now dominate the local market. In addition, they are cutting their teeth in the estimated $110 billion international rolling-stock market, moving into several developing countries where the Chinese government funds railway modernization projects. The combination of low manufacturing costs and modern technologies is helping them make inroads in developed markets too, with CNR recently winning contracts in Australia and New Zealand.

The Chinese government sometimes synchronizes its desire to accelerate growth in a particular sector with the imposition of new regulations on multinationals in that sector. For example, from 1996 to 2005 foreign companies held a 75% share of the Chinese market for wind energy projects. Then the government decided to grow the market dramatically, offering buyers large new subsidies and other incentives. At the same time, it quietly increased the local-content requirement on wind turbines from 40% to 70% and substantially hiked the tariffs on imported components. As the market exploded, foreign manufacturers were unable to expand their supply chains quickly and meet the increased demand. Their Chinese competitors, who had been licensing technology mainly from small European turbine producers, took up the slack rapidly and cost-effectively. By 2009 Chinese companies, led by Sinovel and Goldwind, controlled more than two-thirds of the market. In fact, foreign companies haven't won a single central government–funded wind energy project since 2005.

Beijing finds it tougher to deal with multinational companies in industries such as information technology. Software development doesn't lend itself to mandatory joint ventures, and China has no state-owned companies that can keep pace with the global leaders. It therefore penalizes multinational companies and favors local players in less direct ways. For instance, although Germany's SAP dominates China's ERP software market, the government gives hefty tax rebates to domestic players such as the Kingdee International Software Group, which has

R&D funding and execution

In both China and the U.S., corporate entities perform most R&D. The difference is that in China, the majority of those entities are owned by the state; in 2009 the government funded 69% of the R&D efforts in the country. By contrast, the U.S. government accounted for only 29% of America's R&D expenditures that year.

R&D funding		R&D execution	
United States	China	United States	China
29% Government	69% Government	10% Government	23% Government
65% Industry	21% Industry	71% Industry	67% Industry
6% Academic/ nonprofit	10% Academic/ nonprofit	19% Academic/ nonprofit	10% Academic/ nonprofit

Sources: Battelle Institude, "Global R&D Funding Forecast," December 22, 2009; *China Economic Quarterly,* Q3, 2006, OECD R&D Statistic, 2009.

become the biggest ERP software supplier to small and medium enterprises in the country. In 2010 the government mandated that foreign companies selling software to state-owned customers must disclose their source codes, although it backed down after vehement protests from global vendors and Western governments. China also issues product standards and specifications that force foreign software suppliers to develop special versions for China, allowing Chinese equipment makers to circumvent Western patents and royalty obligations. For example, the country's wireless and 3G mobile telephone standards, WAPI and TD-SCDMA, will never become global standards, but they give local companies an edge and are hurdles in the path of foreign equipment manufacturers.

China's bottom-up support of the technologies of smaller, non-state-owned companies relies on local and provincial governments' self-interest and corruption, most of which is outside Beijing's control. For instance, Chinese companies have come to dominate the global silicon-wafer-panel business. That resulted from massive, uncoordinated capacity increases by dozens of private companies, aided by low-cost financing and inexpensive land sales. Many provincial officials provided Chinese entrepreneurs with land at below-market prices or even for free. Subsidies are available in the West too, but in China they often take the form of land grants that are larger than what's needed to build a factory. Companies build apartment buildings on the surplus land, the cash flow from which pays for R&D and offsets factory losses. State-owned banks give these companies loans at below-market rates, and sometimes the provincial government reimburses interest payments.

Owing to hypercompetition between Chinese companies, which spilled into overseas markets, the prices of solar panels fell worldwide by about 50% in 2009 and 2010, driving higher-cost Western producers into the red. Germany's Q-Cells, an industry pioneer, slid from an operating profit of 16% of sales in 2008 to an operating loss of 60% of sales the following year. China now exports 95% of its solar panels, and Chinese companies such as Suntech, Yingli, and JA Solar control half of the German market and a third of the U.S. market.

So far the Chinese government's technology policy has produced mixed results. In areas such as rail and wind, Chinese companies have replaced multinational corporations in the domestic market, are boosting exports, and are making profits. It's too early to tell in businesses such as jet aircraft manufacture and power generation, where Chinese enterprises lag well behind Western market leaders. In other sectors, such as solar panels, profits are scarce, and foreign rivals with higher-tech products are price competitive and more profitable. China's silicon foundries are unable to compete with sophisticated Taiwanese and South Korean producers, and among the country's computer hardware manufacturers, for instance, only Lenovo and TechFaith, a mobile phone designer, have gained any traction.

Is Conflict Inevitable?

China's policies raise the issue of whether economies with disparate objectives and at different stages of development can coexist without conflict. Tensions between China and the U.S., in particular, are growing, and something has to give if the two nations are to avoid a nasty confrontation soon. The likelihood of conflict depends on the governments of the two countries. The good news is that both of them appear to be pragmatic, operate by consensus at the top, and seem unlikely to commit to self-destructive policies. The two governments also want trade flows between their countries to keep increasing, because people and companies on both sides of the Pacific count on them for wealth and power. Besides, the Chinese government isn't a monolithic body; many senior officials in the Communist Party want the renminbi to appreciate, would like to gain control over opportunistic local officials, and hope to reduce environmental problems.

However, China and the U.S. are structurally prone to economic conflict. They differ radically in their beliefs, expectations, and objectives because of their histories, economic and political systems, and policies. For instance, China regards the management of trade and investment flows as a legitimate way to regain its global leadership, while the U.S. believes the state should play a limited role. Connecting these two systems has reinforced imbalances rather than bringing about equilibrium.

There's a link between China's rapid development and America's slowing growth. China has only about a tenth the capital stock of the U.S., in per capita terms, so it invests roughly three times more, as a percentage of GDP, than the U.S. does. It funds these investments from government surpluses and the profits of state-owned enterprises, by minimizing health care and pension safety nets, and by preventing its savers from accessing investment opportunities abroad. There's also a difference in expectations about future benefits: China is inclined to save more today, while the U.S. prefers current consumption. Despite the postrecession increase in the household savings rate, the U.S. government continues to borrow to maintain consumption levels. It keeps interest rates low, supports current consumer spending, enlarges its net debtor status—and compromises its future growth. Meanwhile, China has invested heavily in manufacturing to cater to this consumption. To keep prices low, it pegs the renminbi to the dollar by limiting currency holdings outside China and requiring exporters to sell their dollars to the central bank. Instead of selling surplus dollars on the foreign exchange market, China's central bank uses them to purchase U.S. debt, keeping the renminbi's exchange rate low and the U.S. economy ticking.

China faces policy rigidities. The Communist Party's ability to remain in power depends on maintaining the rapid growth of the economy and making larger capital investments. The popular view in China is that both trends will continue, that Beijing is doing the right things, and that foreign complaints are de facto attacks on the country. Many economists fear that the government is turning its back on the forces that brought China to where it is today, but its leaders see state capitalism and the containment of foreign companies as China's best chance of regaining technological superiority. As noted earlier, Beijing has little control over local and provincial policies, which deliver most of the subsidies to exporters. Local tax revenues are calculated in relation to sales, not profits, and officials are promoted according to how much employment they generate. This incentive structure for decision makers reinforces the creation of excess capacity, leading to lower prices, which spill over into export markets and irk the U.S.

The U.S. and China do have common interests, such as developing clean energy, protecting the environment, and reining in rogue states. However, an agenda of cooperation between disparate and conflicting systems brings problems. Working with the other side is beneficial but not a core objective, so if the U.S. values cooperation more than China does, it may compromise its interests during negotiations. It might be useful for the U.S. to dispense with the premise that it can have an economically compatible relationship with China. That would clarify China's development strategy and its adverse effects on Western interests, thus brightening the lines the U.S. simply cannot allow China to cross.

It's not clear what will alleviate the structural problems. Changes in China's economic policies are unlikely to happen soon, and counting on them only delays coming to grips with the issue. Although most people anticipate that the Chinese and U.S. systems will eventually become more similar, they are likely to remain fundamentally different until China gets bigger and much richer—and more technologically sophisticated.

There will be no shortage of crises along the way, especially because China "manages" its foreign policy by pressuring rivals. America's challenge, in addition to raising U.S. saving and investment rates, is to overcome its passive reliance on markets and develop aggressive public development strategies of its own. The U.S. either misread what would happen or undervalued its own economic interests while integrating China into the global system. Five years ago Robert Zoellick, then the U.S. deputy secretary of state and now the president of the World Bank, stated with confidence, "[U.S.] policy has succeeded remarkably well: The dragon emerged and joined the world." Perhaps, but in the process the U.S. may have gotten more than it bargained for.

Succeeding in the New China

Multinational corporations must adjust to the growing tensions between China and the U.S. on their own; they operate across national boundaries and cannot wait for balancing macroeconomic forces or multilateral solutions. The Chinese government constantly tests the resolve of foreign companies, but many can't complain. The state pays less attention than it once did to consumer product giants such as Procter & Gamble, Unilever, and Yum Brands. These corporations have been selling in China for so long that consumers regard the brands as local, and their top management teams are chockablock with Chinese executives. However, the state is becoming more intrusive in some ways. By stopping Coca-Cola's acquisition of Huiyuan Juice in 2009, for instance, the government showed that it would protect promising local companies and brands. As for mid-tech manufacturers, such as Otis Elevator, Emerson Electric, and Danaher, they are of little strategic interest to Beijing and will continue to flourish in China.

But the government has fundamentally changed the game for technology-rich companies. China is a big market for them; many operate dozens of subsidiaries and employ tens of thousands of people there. It's also a learning space: The market's complexity and rapid development have already prompted these companies to locate more R&D facilities and develop products in China. The government's new policies will accelerate this trend, forcing companies to bring cutting-edge R&D into the country earlier than they might have

Whose R&D Will Deliver Results?

ARE CHINA'S R&D EFFORTS as productive as America's? Creative destruction is a major force in U.S. business: A company now on the S&P 500 can hope to stay there for 15 years—half the life expectancy in 1990. In China, the corporate pecking order is more apt to change because of state-sponsored mergers than competition. That fact alone suggests that America's R&D is more productive than China's.

China's most innovative technologies have come from privately owned companies, such as the electric automobile maker BYD, the telecom firm Huawei, and the solar panel manufacturer Suntech. However, 40 of the 50 Chinese companies with the largest R&D expenditures are state owned; they will have to become more innovative if China is to catch up to the U.S. And catching up isn't the same as keeping up.

Of course, the U.S. has problems, too. Government funding of basic research has been flat, in real terms, since 1995, and the U.S. is falling behind in areas such as clean energy and water. In addition, the common U.S. practice of awarding narrowly focused, short duration federal research grants underperforms the establishment of multi disciplinary teams that stay together. Still, the U.S. may well respond to the Chinese challenge once that challenge becomes widely known—as it successfully did to the Soviet space program in the 1960s.

planned and on different terms than they would have liked. Still, these companies' best response would be to continue making themselves indispensable to the Chinese government, state-owned partners, and customers.

Western corporations have much that China needs. For example, IBM is helping to build a "smart" railway-management system for the state-owned metro in

Guangzhou City. Similarly, GE, because of its knowledge of aviation technology, was able to negotiate a partnership with Aviation Industry Corporation of China in 2009 for the development of commercial aircraft. GE would have liked full control of the venture, as it enjoys elsewhere, but that's unlikely in China. Multinationals have the strongest hand with authorities when they have a technology that China wants and no one else has. In 2007 the French company Areva successfully rebuffed Premier Wen Jiabao's attempt to force it to transfer its unique nuclear-fuel-recycling technology as part of a $12 billion nuclear reactor deal. But this was a rare exception; China usually wins.

The most technology-rich multinationals can gain direct access to China's leaders, who find it more efficient to deal with the CEOs who own the technologies they want than with their governments, who like to scold. Former CEOs Hank Greenberg of AIG and Bill Gates of Microsoft are cases in point. Greenberg started cultivating China's leaders in the 1970s, buying and returning stolen Chinese works of art, and 25 years later the Chinese government rewarded AIG with special privileges when it opened the insurance market to foreign companies. Gates, after some early struggles, warmed to the challenge, looked past the software piracy in China, and learned to work with Beijing. In return, the government forced PC manufacturers in the country to load legal software onto their computers and required the computers it bought to have legal software. The Chinese have long memories; they admire the time horizons of CEOs like Greenberg and Gates.

Many multinational companies have long collaborated with state-owned enterprises to create stronger business positions than either could have achieved on its own. Cummins is an equal partner in both production and R&D with its largest Chinese diesel engine customer, Dongfeng Motor. This has allowed the U.S. corporation to develop products in China faster than it otherwise could have and to strike relationships with new customers, such as urban mass-transit operators, that value Cummins above other suppliers. All this has helped Cummins's facilities outside China sell four times as many products in China as they export from the country.

Global forces have catalyzed new forms of cooperation between Chinese companies and foreign corporations. Many products sold in emerging markets have different design requirements from similar products used in developed countries, and China, the world's largest developing country, is often the best place to develop them. For instance, Shanghai Automotive Industry Corporation and Volkswagen's 50/50 joint venture has designed a car that it will license to both partners for sale in other emerging markets, and Shanghai Auto has formed a venture with its other partner, GM, to serve India's car market. In fact, teaming up with Chinese companies is becoming essential for multinational corporations wishing to compete cost-effectively in emerging markets. New entrants in the global power industry, such as (South) Korea Electric Power, have shrunk the odds that Western companies will win bids in developing countries unless they source from China.

More collaboration options are available than ever before, and the Chinese government, through its aid budgets, policies, and support of business deals, is influencing how the new order will evolve.

Already multinational companies have learned to better protect their intellectual property in China. They split cutting-edge technology between different partners, post more employees from home to handle sensitive work, and build stronger personal and organizational links with their partners. They negotiate with the government over such things as the use of their technology, which officials will see it, and which jurisdiction will settle any legal disputes.

Protests by Western governments can moderate only the most aggressive of China's policy initiatives. A global re-alignment of business is under way. It includes the spread of competitive capability to China and other emerging markets, a surge of investment in those countries, and a shift of wealth and business platforms from developed to developing economies. If they wish to remain global technology leaders, Western corporations—which are more innovative than slow, debt-ridden governments and Chinese state-owned enterprises—must bring to bear greater imagination as they search for growth, collaboration, and advantage.

THOMAS M. HOUT is a visiting professor at the University of Hong Kong's School of Business. **PANKAJ GHEMAWAT** is the Anselmo Rubiralta Chair of Global Strategy at IESE Business School in Barcelona.

Originally published in December 2010. Reprint R1012H

Is It Too Late to Enter China?

by Edward Tse

IS NOW A SMART TIME to enter or expand in China? On the one hand, the answer seems like a no-brainer. While many other countries have slipped into an economic coma, China is humming along, with Goldman Sachs projecting that the economy will grow by more than 11% in 2010. On the other hand, these are not happy times for many foreign investors. The clash between Google and the Chinese government, along with the ongoing vulnerability of intellectual property rights and continuing restrictions on foreign ownership in China, makes CEOs wonder if a presence there is worth the risks.

In a recent article in *Time,* James McGregor, a consultant and former chairman of the American Chamber of Commerce in China, voiced some of the problems vexing foreign investors: competition from inexpensive knockoffs; rivalry from state-owned enterprises that enjoy special advantages; and seemingly duplicitous government policies such as the selective enforcement of World Trade Organization norms. McGregor wrote that CEOs are "losing sleep over expectations that their onetime [Chinese] partners are morphing into predators—and that their own technology and know-how will be coming back at them globally in the form of cut-price products from subsidized state-owned behemoths." There's also a growing perception that the Chinese government has hardened its attitude toward the outside world, blaming the United States for creating the global financial crisis, and favoring local companies over foreign ones.

These challenges are real, but they aren't new—and they certainly don't tell the full story. To enter a complex country like China without understanding the context is folly. Although the Chinese government began freeing the economy from controls in 1978, it has always wielded a strong hand over business, balancing the need for economic growth—and the entrepreneurship that demands—with its overriding desire to maintain political and social stability. The government still prevents foreign companies from entering core sectors such as telecommunications and media. It has also re-structured and rejuvenated state-owned companies, including Baosteel, Industrial and Commercial Bank of China, China National Petroleum, and China Mobile. They are becoming fierce competitors, particularly since they enjoy government backing.

In the sectors that any company may enter, China is awash with competitors, both local and foreign. Look at the figures. The number of private companies in China shot up from 140,000 in 1992 to 6.6 million by the end of 2008, even as the number of foreign corporations

Idea in Brief

China grew by 8.5% in 2009 and is poised to expand by more than 11% in 2010. That makes it a wonderfully attractive market. But it is also the most competitive and complex market on the planet. Chinese and foreign companies battle ferociously in almost every industry, and profit margins are lower there than anywhere else. Moreover, the Chinese government can intervene whenever it wants to and does so in unpredictable ways—as the January 2010 tussle with Google demonstrated. Some might think that only the brave or the foolhardy would rush into the country, but the author disagrees, claiming that no company can afford to ignore China anymore. In fact, he argues, CEOs have to integrate their China business with their international operations, so that the country can provide them with a global competitive advantage. Companies that don't make the shift will be elbowed aside by those that use China to transform their competitive positions.

grew to 435,000. Of the *Fortune* 500 companies, about 480 are already in China, according to its government. This makes for a marketplace in which Chinese and foreign companies battle for survival. Several surveys report that profits are slowly rising but that most multinationals still find it tough to earn the margins they can realize at home. Indeed, many enterprises and entrepreneurs believe that soon it might be too late to enter China successfully.

Although it may be scary to consider entering what is arguably the world's most complicated and competitive market, the notion that it isn't necessary to do so is misguided. Few Western companies were prepared for the speed of China's recovery; fewer still are ready to handle the fact that China will soon be the world's growth engine in terms of output and consumption. Consider two pieces of evidence. One, China surpassed the U.S. as the world's largest automotive market in 2009. Two, according to a September 2009 report from the China Enterprise Confederation and the China Enterprise Directors Association, the top 500 Chinese companies' net profits were $170.6 billion in the first half of 2009, exceeding for the first time the net profits reported by the top 500 American companies, which were $98.9 billion for that period. Not only will China replace the United States as the world's largest economy faster than predicted, but China's (and India's) growth may make Asia the source of about 50% of the world's gross domestic product by 2030.

At the same time, doing business in China doesn't mean what it used to. Many companies believe they have figured out how to operate there, but the scale and intensity of change in the Chinese economy is rendering even successful strategies inadequate. It is no longer sufficient to develop a freestanding business in the country. In most industries, China is becoming a game changer, with companies' operations there altering the basis of competition the world over. CEOs must therefore develop a new China strategy—one that isn't simply a plan for selling in or sourcing from China. They must integrate the China business with their operations elsewhere, so that China can provide them with a global competitive advantage. I call this a one-world strategy with China at its core.

Making the transition will be difficult even for companies that have operated in China for decades. But those that don't make the shift will be pushed aside by rivals, old and new, that are already using China to transform their competitive positions—as I will show in the following pages.

The China Context

Executives usually consider three *c*'s when formulating strategy: customers, competitors, and the company. As I suggested earlier, they must add one more for China: context. That's easier said than done; three factors keep changing the context in China.

Official China

Despite recent controversy over the Communist Party of China's attitude toward foreign companies, economic liberalization will continue. Growth generates legitimacy for China's government and guarantees social stability. However, the party will continue to determine the pace at which it frees the economy from controls. Companies that wish to do business in China must understand the government's priorities and modify their strategies accordingly. The government has retained ownership of key companies in the communications, energy, finance, resources, and media sectors, and contrary to foreign investors' hopes, it has no intention of letting go of them in the near future.

A handful of companies may eventually decide, as Google did, that China just isn't right for them. Google entered the Chinese market in early 2000 by creating a Chinese-language version of its home page. Because the facilities were located on U.S. soil, Google wasn't subject to Chinese censorship laws and didn't need a license from the Chinese government to operate its business. In 2004 Google realized that rivals such as Yahoo and Microsoft were getting ahead because they had established a presence in China. In January 2006, after a year of preparation, the company announced the creation of Google.cn, located in China and subject to Chinese filtering.

The decision to physically enter China and expose search results to censorship drew a lot of criticism, and Google has been of two minds about the decision since then. The company had to decide whether to "compromise our mission by failing to serve our users in China or compromise our mission by entering China and complying with Chinese laws that require us to censor search results," a Google spokesperson said at the time. "Self-censorship, like that which we are now required to perform in China, is something that conflicts deeply with our core principles. . . . This was not something we did enthusiastically or something that we're proud of at all."

Google's January 2010 announcement that it would close its China operations if the government didn't lift censorship wasn't surprising. Like almost all the Western internet majors, Google has found competing with Chinese companies difficult. Yahoo has long since opted for a minority stake in a joint venture with China's successful business portal, Alibaba.com, in a market dominated by Sohu.com, the leading online media company. Because China's online auction market is dominated by Taobao.com, eBay hasn't done very well either. A lot of money will be made in China's internet market, but it will go mostly to domestic companies that are better able to handle the political intricacies of running such businesses in China. And Google hasn't yet left China— at least not at the time of this writing. It used its announcement to clarify its views, to publicize its concerns about cyberattacks, and to open talks with government representatives. The company is still trying to establish a position in the Chinese context, knowing that if it can find a way to manage the reputational risks, maintaining its China operation will not be a bad thing.

Google may not succeed, because its business touches on one of Beijing's most sensitive areas: politically related debate, which the party insists on controlling. In other sectors, though, the potential benefits outweigh the risks. For example, foreign carmakers are restricted to joint ventures in which their maximum stake is 50%. This limitation is balanced by the possibility of selling products in the world's largest automobile market and gaining unmatchable economies of scale. Even five years ago it could be argued that the unknowns of entering China made delaying a decision to do so worthwhile. Since then its business environment has become more accessible and transparent, so companies that continue to hesitate may find it difficult to break into the Chinese market in the future.

Many Westerners believe that where economic freedoms lead, political freedoms must follow. They're wrong. China will remain a communist nation in the near future. The party's 75 million members, who dominate government and society, believe that China's development can take place only under its leadership. Although

Beijing recognizes that the rest of the world expects it to play a leadership role, it is having a tough time balancing global expectations with the desire to follow former party leader Deng Xiaoping's doctrine that China must keep a low profile. This tension results in outsiders' believing that the Chinese government is arrogant, whereas it is merely undecided about how much attention it should pay to the world outside the Wall when it has so many challenges to tackle at home.

Competitive China

Many executives take for granted that China—compared with, say, Russia and India, or even Japan and South Korea—has an open marketplace. Unlike Asia's other economies, China opened its markets to foreign companies when its economic reforms began and has opened them wider ever since. It spawns the world's largest number of start-ups; is growing global giants such as Lenovo, Haier, Huawei, and ZTE; and attracts the most foreign companies, too. That results in intense competition and creates a host of business opportunities in China, particularly for forging alliances and partnerships.

Large investments and cheap labor have propelled economic growth in China until now, leading to enormous waste and environmental damage. Over the next decade government policy will drive a switch to efficiency and conservation. Companies in China will have to reduce their consumption of raw materials, mitigate the environmental impact of their operations, radically improve quality, and hone their management skills.

That will make them even more competitive than they are today.

Consumer China

The money generated by China's growth has created a substantial middle class. As a result, no other country—not even Japan or the United States—has as many products and brands as China does. This has resulted in a lack of brand loyalty and quick shifts in market share. Chinese consumers have become as diverse in their tastes as their Western counterparts, and they're just as demanding.

In addition, China is changing from a largely rural nation to one of cities. By 2020 city dwellers will account for 60% of the population, compared with 40% in 2009, and new metropolitan areas will form across the country. The migration of 200 million people will transform markets afresh: Urban consumers differ from rural ones in the products and services they want. Over the next 10 years China's mass market will morph into differentiated and multitiered segments. Because these new markets will be linked with one another, with the coastal areas, and with the rest of the world by a reliable transport and communications infrastructure, they will be far easier to reach than they were five years ago.

Thus executives who believe that the Chinese government is welcoming but opaque should regard it as a powerful player on the world stage. Those who have been treating China's companies as suppliers must treat them as potential competitors. And those who have

China's scorching pace of growth

The recent recession seems to have been just a temporary setback for China.

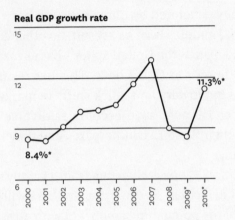

Real GDP growth rate

*Projected
Source: IMF WEO

been approaching China as a mass market would do well to approach it as a collection of different consumer segments. Because of the size of the market and the reach of the corporations in it, almost every company must compete, at least in some form, in China.

Five Questions for Shaping a China Strategy

To fashion a China strategy that can ride these forces, executives must answer five questions. These questions apply to most industries and situations; they're based on my two decades of experience in helping foreign companies enter China.

The growth of outside investment

In seven years foreign companies more than doubled their investment in China.

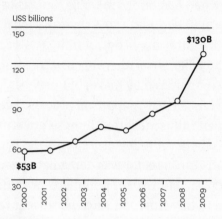

US$ billions

$130B

$53B

Source: Booz & Company

The first three help establish where companies are in relation to China's economic development.

How open is—and will be—our industry in China?

The Chinese government imposes legal restrictions on both the nature of corporate ownership and the products and services that companies may offer. Although the state is opening up more industries to competition, it doesn't follow a timetable. Companies must monitor the extent to which—and the pace at which—the government frees industries from controls. It's important to bag a license the moment an industry is deregulated, so companies in sectors that are currently closed should build connections (*guanxi*) with key officials as a source of competitive advantage.

Few sectors in China are completely off-limits, but the rules can be complex. For example, both foreign automobile companies and foreign banks are permitted to set up fully owned operations in China, but, as I stated earlier, the former may hold a 50% share in a local company, whereas the latter may control only 25% of a Chinese bank's equity. Moreover, there are few constraints on the cars that companies may make, but new banking products often face a lengthy approval process. Even in completely open industries, the Chinese government will intervene whenever it deems it necessary. For instance, China's soft-drinks sector was deregulated decades ago, but in 2009 the Ministry of Commerce wouldn't permit Coca-Cola to buy Huiyuan Juice because it feared that the takeover would reduce competition.

What business models should we use?

Foreign companies' business models fall into two categories: *sourcing-centric* and *sales-centric*. Enterprises using the former, particularly in sectors such as consumer electronics and mobile communications, have established export bases in China, but their local marketing and sales capabilities are limited. Those deploying the latter, particularly in the fast-moving consumer goods and automotive industries, focus on the Chinese market.

Smart companies combine the two models as they expand. For example, they design some product lines both for China's wealthiest consumers and for export to the developed world, while aiming less-expensive products at a broader range of consumers in China's upper-tier markets—large, cosmopolitan cities such as Shanghai, Beijing, and Guangzhou. Some of these companies also offer a third set of products to frugal consumers who are adjusting to urban life in China's middle-tier cities. Managing multiple business models is tough but often necessary to cash in on the opportunities in China.

Can we live with China's uncertainties?

The pace of change, lack of data, and high executive turnover in China render decision making hard for foreign companies. Nevertheless, it's better to be approximately right than precisely wrong. Anticipating specific changes is impossible, but leaders should be ready to act when opportunities or new constraints appear.

Many Chinese chief executives thrive under these conditions, so it's a good idea to learn from them. Haier's Zhang Ruimin and Hauwei's Ren Zhengfei, for instance, don't succeed by trying to get things right all the time. They are fearless experimenters who are willing to learn, launch, adapt, and improve in quick bursts. The Chinese market demands managers who see things in a nonlinear fashion and can act boldly when necessary.

However, it's a good idea for foreign companies to temper opportunism with experience. For instance, many experts saw Toyota as a latecomer and a slow mover in China. Volkswagen and GM established joint ventures with prestigious local companies and racked up large market shares before the Japanese company teamed up with Guangzhou Auto, in 2004. However, because its partner was a relative lightweight, Toyota learned more about doing business in China and gained greater control over the venture than its rivals had. By 2008 Toyota was China's largest car company by revenue (110 billion yuan versus Volkswagen's 96 billion yuan) and the second largest by sales (525,000 cars to Volkswagen's 760,000).

The two remaining questions enable companies to develop a one-world strategy with China at its core.

How can we integrate our China operations with our businesses elsewhere in the world?

The stand-alone business models that many multinational companies have been using in China are coming under pressure from rising costs—particularly those of labor and raw materials—as well as the yuan's appreciation. The rise of the yuan stopped in the second half of 2008, largely because of the global financial crisis, but its value is bound to increase in the future. In order to keep costs down, companies will have to integrate their China operations with their businesses elsewhere—for instance, by developing products in China and manufacturing them in other Asian countries—and vice versa. This will make management more complex, but it will be essential if these enterprises are to remain globally competitive.

Some companies, such as Coca-Cola and Nokia, have started by setting up R&D laboratories and product development centers in China so that they can tap into the large supply of engineers and scientists in the country. These companies develop products by combining insights into the Chinese consumer with global platforms and then finding markets outside the country for those innovations. For instance, a little more than half of the handsets Nokia develops in China are sold in other countries. A.O. Smith, the American water heater manufacturer, has introduced in the U.S. products designed in China and is using some of its Chinese manufacturing capacity to make water heaters for the Indian market. In 2008 A.O. Smith China attained a 33% growth rate and ranked second only to Haier in the Chinese market.

Can we move more parts of our value chain to China?
The relocation of value-creation activity to China has gone through several stages. The first involved setting up manufacturing facilities there, and the second involved making China a major sourcing location. In the third stage, which began in the early 2000s, companies incorporated their China facilities into their global manufacturing networks even as they started building distribution networks to reach China's prosperous regions. In the fourth stage, companies are making China a key part of their value chains. This entails moving some operations from headquarters to China. For example, by monitoring research labs, enterprises are drawing on Chinese R&D as it matures. They are also extending their value chains from China. Global networks of suppliers have grown to include foreign companies operating in China as well as Chinese companies and entities funded by Chinese investors.

These two trends, increased R&D and the development of global value chains, favor enterprises that locate each element—from research, through manufacturing,

---

5 questions to ask before investing in China

1. How open is—and will be—our industry in China?

2. What business models should we use?

3. Can we live with China's uncertainties?

4. How can we integrate our China operations with our business elsewhere in the world?

5. Can we move more parts of our value chain to China?

---

sourcing, and procurement, to distribution and marketing—in the most appropriate place. Such one-world companies can take advantage of China's growing markets, its increasing dominance of parts of the value chain, its talent pools, and its integration with global communications and transport networks. They will protect themselves against intellectual property theft by developing highly innovative product designs, keeping some of their operations closely guarded, and providing customer service of a quality that is difficult to imitate. A few multinationals have already made this shift. Among them are Nokia—which treats China as its main manufacturing base, a major market, and a primary source of new handset designs—and Samsung, which earmarked $1 billion in 2009 to develop more products and expand its operations in the country.

Honeywell, too, has developed a strategy that turns on its head the traditional approach of developing industrial controls in the United States and selling them to the rest of the world. In 2003 the company relocated its Asia-Pacific headquarters from Hong Kong to Shanghai, and in 2007 it opened a global engineering center in Chongqing and transferred the headquarters of its electronic materials division to Shanghai. From 2003 to 2009 Honeywell more than doubled its China staff to around 9,000 people, with a number of new hires going to work in a 1,000-person R&D center in Shanghai. Honeywell has developed several new products in China. Some of them have fewer functions than its U.S. range, others have the same functions, and still others are entirely new. The company designed these industrial controls mainly for Chinese customers, but it is exporting them to other parts of the world as well. They sell for less, on average, than Honeywell's traditional range, but owing to lower development and production costs, the company earns higher margins on them. Honeywell has protected its intellectual property by manufacturing quality products and building a strong brand. Local competitors' products are not only markedly inferior but also just as expensive as Honeywell's versions. Its revenues in China rose fivefold from 2004 to 2009.

Leaders of companies that don't have operations in China today are bound to feel handicapped, but they shouldn't make the mistake of thinking they have been left too far behind. China's integration with the global economy is increasing, and the changes the country is undergoing have created a bewildering array of possibilities. Latecomers can set up globally integrated businesses from the outset, which will transform them worldwide. In fact, that's an opportunity they are best placed to exploit.

EDWARD TSE is the chairman of Booz & Company, Greater China.

Originally published in April 2010. Reprint R1004J

How Local Companies Keep Multinationals at Bay

by Arindam K. Bhattacharya and David C. Michael

SINCE THE LATE 1970S, governments on every continent have allowed the winds of global competition to blow through their economies. As policy makers have lowered tariff barriers and permitted foreign investments, multinational companies have rushed into those countries. U.S., European, and Japanese giants, it initially appeared, would quickly overrun local rivals and grab the market for almost every product or service. After all, they possessed state-of-the-art technologies and products, enormous financial resources, powerful brands, and the world's best management talent and systems. Poor nations such as Brazil, China, India, and Mexico, often under pressure from developed countries, let in trans-national companies, but they did so slowly, almost reluctantly. They were convinced that global Goliaths would wipe out local enterprises in one fell swoop.

That hasn't happened, according to our research. Over the past three years, we have been studying companies in 10 rapidly developing economies: Brazil, China, India, Indonesia, Malaysia, Mexico, Poland, Russia, Slovakia, and Thailand. In those countries, smart domestic enterprises are more than holding their own in the face of foreign competition. They have staved off challenges from multinational corporations in their core businesses, have become market leaders or are catching up with them, and have often seized new opportunities before foreign players could. Many of them dominate the market today not because of protectionist economic policies, but because of their strategies and execution. When we drew up a list of 50 homegrown champions, we found that 21 had revenues exceeding US$1 billion in 2006 and that the entire group's sales had risen by about 50% between 2005 and 2006 (see the exhibit "Fifty homegrown champions"). The skeptics should have remembered that David slew Goliath—not the other way around.

Consider a few local companies that have fended off foreign competition during the past five years or more:

- In Brazil, Grupo Positivo has a larger share of the PC market than either Dell or Hewlett-Packard, and Totvs is the enterprise resource planning (ERP) software leader in the small- and midsize-company market, ahead of the world's largest business software provider, SAP.

Idea in Brief

If you're setting out to compete in rapidly developing economies, beware: Smart domestic enterprises are staving off the challenge from global market leaders. And they're seizing new opportunities before multinationals can.

Consider: In China, search engine Baidu is used seven times more than Google China every day. In India, Bharti Airtel has trumped Vodafone as the market leader in cellular telephony. And in Mexico, Grupo Elektra has beaten Wal-Mart as the country's top retailer.

Domestic dynamos like these dominate foreign rivals by applying six strategies. For example, they use their deep understanding of consumers in their countries to create highly customized offerings. They leverage cutting-edge technology to keep operating costs down. And they tap into pools of cheap local labor instead of relying on expensive automation.

To prevail over local winners on their turf, set aside your tried-and-true strategies, advise Bhattacharya and Michael. Instead, understand—and emulate—domestic players' tactics.

- In China, daily use of the search engine Baidu exceeds that of Google China by fourfold; QQ, from instant-message leader Tencent, is ahead of MSN Messenger; and online travel service Ctrip has held off Travelsky, Expedia's eLong.com, and Travelocity's Zuji.com.

- In India, Bharti Airtel has taken on Hutchison Telecom, which sold its Indian operations to Vodafone in 2007, and emerged as the leader in the cellular telephone market.

- In Mexico, Grupo Elektra, which has created one of the country's biggest retail networks, has taken the battle to Wal-Mart.

Idea in Practice

Bhattacharya and Michael identify a blend of six strategies domestic winners use to succeed in emerging markets.

Create Customized Offerings

Simple customization techniques, based on intimate knowledge of local consumers, have sparked major success for homegrown champions.

Example: India's CavinKare packages shampoo in single-use sachets, making the product affordable for Indians who can't afford big bottles and regard shampoo as a luxury. CavinKare is the largest local player in India's $500 million shampoo industry.

Develop Business Models to Overcome Obstacles

Smart local companies identify key challenges posed by domestic markets, then design business models to overcome them.

Example: Shanda has avoided the software piracy problem plaguing global video-game leaders in China by developing highly popular multiplayer online role-playing games. These are impossible to pirate, because they're live experiences created by many players over the Internet.

Deploy Cutting-Edge Technologies

Local winners use new technology to control operating costs and deliver quality offerings.

Example: Brazil's Gol Linhas Aereas Inteligentes (Gol), South America's first low-cost airline, uses the latest model Boeing 737 in its single-model fleet. The young fleet requires less maintenance, so Gol manages quick turnarounds, which lowers cost per available seat. Gol's use of e-tickets and unmanned check-in kiosks has further driven down costs.

Tap Low-Cost Labor

Local champions leverage cheap labor pools rather than relying on automation.

- In Russia, Wimm-Bill-Dann Foods is the biggest producer of dairy products, ahead of Danone and Coca-Cola.

Example: China's largest outdoor advertising firm, Focus Media, has installed LCD screens in 130,000 locations in 90 cities. Instead of linking the screens electronically through expensive technology, it uses employees who go from building to building on bicycles to replace advertisement DVDs. This decreases operating costs, enabling the company to offer advertisers immense flexibility cheaply.

Build Scale Quickly

Successful local companies fend off multinationals and other regional players by rapidly expanding their reach.

Example: Focus Media initially faced many rivals across China. To gain nationwide reach, it pursued an aggressive acquisition-led strategy. Its national coverage attracted advertisers, diminished regional rivals' competitiveness, and vaulted it past two global leaders involved in China's outdoor advertising industry.

Use Management Talent to Sustain Growth

To avoid the problems that can come with high growth, domestic dynamos put the right management talent in place.

Example: Russia's Wimm-Bill-Dann Foods, founded by five entrepreneurs with borrowed funds, changed its management structure when multinationals began encroaching on its local dairy and fruit-juice markets. The founders hired a new CEO with extensive industry experience and gave him free rein. They also brought in seasoned managers from multinational companies. WBD now has 34% of the Russian market for packaged dairy products.

The local companies' success doesn't augur well for the developed world's corporations, many of which are seeking growth and profits in emerging markets.

Fifty homegrown champions

Using a largely qualitative approach, we identified successful domestic companies in 10 emerging economies. We chose enterprises that generate almost all their revenues from their home markets and that have been (or are close to being) leaders in their main businesses. Below is a list of 50 companies that we studied in depth; it is neither a ranking nor an exhaustive catalog of homegrown winners.

	Company	2006 net revenues (in US$ millions)	2006 net revenue growth (% change from 2005)	Domestic market position	Main foreign rivals in local market
Brazil	B2W	72B	63%	largest online retailer	fnac.com
	Casas Bahia	5,024	not available	biggest consumer electronics and furniture retailer	Carrefour, Wal-Mart
	Cosan	1,083	30%	largest manufacturer and seller of ethanol and sugar	Bunge, Cargill
	Gol Linhas Aéreas Inteligentes	1,661	42%	second-biggest and fastest-growing airline	none on domestic routes
	Grupo Positivo	507	89%	leader in PCs and notebooks	Dell, Hewlett-Packard, Lenovo
	o Boticário	1,321	4%	one of the largest cosmetics brands	Avon, Revlon
	Totvs	164	21%	leading ERP-solutions provider for medium and small companies	SAP
	TV Globo	2,732	12%	number one television network	none
	Votorantim Finanças	533	9%	third-largest automobile finance company	Citibank, Grupo Santander, HSBC

Company	2006 net revenues (in USS millions)	2006 net revenue growth (% change from 2005)	Domestic market position	Main foreign rivals in local market
Baidu	104	163%	China's most-used internet search engine	Google China
China Merchants Bank	3,081	29%	one of the top 10 banks	local banks with foreign partners
China Vanke	2,103	70%	largest property developer	joint ventures with foreign partners
Ctrip	97	49%	biggest provider of hotel and flight bookings	eLong.com (Expedia), Zuji.com (Travelocity)
Focus Media	206	213%	largest outdoor advertising company	Clear Channel, JCDecaux
Goldwind Science and Technology	190	209%	biggest maker and seller of wind-power equipment	GE, Vestas
Gome Electrical Appliances	3,064	38%	largest home-appliances retail chain	Best Buy, Carrefour, Wal-Mart
Goodbaby	327	14%	largest seller of baby products	Chicco, Maclaren
New Oriental Education & Technology	129	36%	leader in language education	Wall Street Institute
Shanda	205	13%	leader in online games	Electronic Arts, Nintendo, Sony
SIM Technology Group	440	26%	largest handset-design house	Bellwave, Compal
Tencent	347	96%	leader in instant messaging	MSN, MySpace

(continued)

71

Fifty homegrown champions (*continued*)

	Company	2006 net revenues (in US$ millions)	2006 net revenue growth (% change from 2005)	Domestic market position	Main foreign rivals in local market
China	WuXi PharmaTech	68	107%	biotech and pharmaceuticals contract R&D leader	Covance
	XinAo Group	1,081	40%	largest gas utility	Hong Kong and China Gas Company
	Xinyi Glass	249	40%	one of the biggest glassmakers	Pilkington
India	Apollo Hospitals	215	23%	largest private hospital chain	joint ventures with foreign partners
	Bharti Airtel	4,162	59%	biggest private-sector telecom services provider	Hutchison Telecom
	CavinKare	129	0.5%	third-largest shampoo maker	L'Oréal, P&G, Unilever
	Gujarat Cooperative Milk Marketing Federation	961	13%	leader in dairy products with its Amul brand	Cadbury, Nestlé, Unilever
	ICICI Bank	5,308	63%	biggest private-sector bank	Citibank, HSBC, Standard Chartered
	The Indian Hotels Company	347	42%	one of the two biggest domestic hotel chains	none
	ITC	2,856	26%	leader in ready-to-cook and other foods	Danone, PepsiCo, Unilever

	Company	2006 net revenues (in US$ millions)	2006 net revenue growth (% change from 2005)	Domestic market position	Main foreign rivals in local market
India	NIIT	179	76%	largest IT education and training firm	Lionbridge
	SKS Micro-finance	7	169%	one of the fastest-growing microfinance groups	none
	Subhiksha	180	140%	largest no-frills super-market chain	none
	Titan Industries	480	44%	largest watch manufacturer and retailer	Citizen, Swatch
Indonesia	Astra International	6,106	10%	biggest car maker (with six foreign partners)	Honda, Mitsubishi, Suzuki
Malaysia	Air Asia	230	28%	one of Asia's fastest-growing low cost airlines	Singapore Airlines
Mexico	Controladora Milano	258(est.)	not available	leading retail apparel chain	Wal-Mart
	Corporación Interamericana de Entretenimiento	944	14%	leading live-entertainment company	none
	Desarrolladora Homex	1,190	46%	largest low-income-housing developer	none
	Farmacia Guadalajara	1,066	13%	second-largest retail pharmaceutical chain	Wal-Mart
	Grupo Elektra	3,270	10%	leading retail network	Wal-Mart
	Sigma Alimentos	1,836	7%	top producer of refrigerated and frozen foods	Danone, Kraft, Nestlé

(continued)

Fifty homegrown champions (*continued*)

	Company	2006 net revenues (in USS millions)	2006 net revenue growth (% change from 2005)	Domestic market position	Main foreign rivals in local market
Poland	**Atlas Group**	282	5%	biggest construction chemicals and glues manufacturer	Henkel
	Maspex Wadowice	634	11%	leader in instant foods, pasta, and fruit juices	Barilla, Cappy
Russia	**Euroset**	4,620	79%	largest mobile telecommunications retailer	none
	MegaFon	3,733	56%	second-biggest cellular services operator	none
	Wimm-Bill-Dann Foods	1,762	26%	leader in dairy products and among the top three in fruit juices	Coca-Cola, Danone
Slovakia	**SkyEurope Airlines**	198	41%	country's biggest airline	easyJet, Ryanair
Thailand	**Siam Cement Group**	6,625	18%	largest maker of building materials, cement, chemicals, and paper	Lafarge

Note: For commercial banks, the figures correspond to operating income. For Indian companies, data are for the fiscal year ending March 31, 2007. Most currency conversions were calculated using the average interbank exchange rate from January 1, 2005, through December 31, 2006.

Two-thirds of respondents to a survey of transnational corporations we conducted in 2006 said they planned to expand their commitments to developing economies over the next five years. That isn't surprising. According to the Economist Intelligence Unit, rapidly developing economies will account for 45% of world GDP and 60% of annual GDP growth by 2010. At the same time, several Western and Japanese corporations have been unable to enter or have retreated from emerging markets. For instance, Yahoo and eBay have pulled out of China, and NEC and Panasonic have withdrawn from the Chinese market for cellular handsets. Other corporations have found it tough to fly down from the premium perches they constructed for themselves, and they no longer appear irresistible to consumers or unbeatable by local companies.

Why don't the strategies of the biggest and brightest corporations work well in developing countries? Part of the problem is that many transnational enterprises mistakenly believe that emerging markets are years behind developed nations' and that the former's markets will eventually look like the latter's. Multinational corporations assume it's merely a matter of time before their existing business models and value propositions start delivering results in developing countries. These misconceptions are deadly—for several reasons.

Developing economies neither are behind developed ones nor show signs of converging with them. The emerging markets are different, behind in some ways and advanced in others. For instance, China's telecommunications infrastructure is newer and better than that in most parts of the United States. At the same time, roughly 300 million Chinese live on less than $1 a day, according to the World Bank. In India, an educated elite who command international wages flourish in a nation with high rates of illiteracy. In Russia, abundant venture capital coexists with murky property rights and intimidating bureaucratic barriers. These disparities aren't likely to disappear soon, and they're creating unique markets.

The obstacles and opportunities that characterize emerging markets render useless most cookie-cutter strategies. A simple example: In India, lack of reliable internet access renders online customer service useless. However, wireless telecommunication networks and widespread use of mobile telephones allow companies to help customers, even in rural areas, through text messages and handset-based internet portals. Only companies that are unfazed by such contradictions are likely to succeed.

Western companies often forget that entrepreneurship has recently exploded in most developing countries because of internal reforms. Governments have slashed red tape, and capital is cheaper than ever—and those changes are stoking competition. Emerging markets have become so volatile that multinational companies can't tackle them with strategies they developed decades ago and have since refined in mature home markets.

Multinational companies should, we believe, borrow a page, or more, from the local champions' playbook. When we analyzed how 50 companies have become winners, we found six common strands—and they aren't all about low-cost structures. One, unlike global companies, local leaders are not constrained by existing products or by preconceived notions about customer needs. They customize products and services to meet different consumer requirements, and they initially go after economies of scope. Two, their business models overcome roadblocks and yield competitive advantages in the process. Three, they turn globalization to their advantage, deploying the latest technologies by developing or buying them. Four, many of the homegrown champions find innovative ways to benefit from low-cost labor pools and to overcome shortages of skilled talent. Five, they go national as soon as possible to prevent regional rivals from challenging them. Finally, the domestic dynamos possess management skills and talent that multinational companies often underestimate.

In the following pages, we explore each of these factors in detail. No single element may seem groundbreaking, but the homegrown champions cleverly weave at least four of them—sometimes all six, as we show—into a tight strategy in order to gain competitive advantage. We also discuss three multinational companies that have followed the six-part path and have tasted success in emerging markets.

A Six-Part Strategy for Success

Many types of local companies have been successful in developing countries. Some are part of old conglomerates owned by business families or tycoons; others are young start-ups spawned by a postreforms generation of entrepreneurs. All the companies we studied face stiff competition from domestic peers or government-owned enterprises. Most of them also face foreign competition at home, even though countries and markets vary in their degree of openness. These domestic private-sector enterprises have outperformed competitors by following several strategies.

Create Customized Products or Services

The homegrown champions possess a deep understanding of the consumers in their countries. They know people's preferences by region or even city, by income level, by age group, and by gender. These companies also grasp the structures of the raw-materials, components, and finished-goods markets in which they operate. They are therefore able to provide consumers with a low level of customization inexpensively. These local leaders develop offerings tailored to several niche markets and learn to create a large variety of products or services cost-effectively. For example, Goodbaby, the leader in the Chinese market for baby-related products such as strollers, sells as many as 1,600 items in 16 categories. Customization becomes the basis on which companies like Goodbaby differentiate themselves from and get a leg up on multinational rivals.

Some companies develop sophisticated user-generated customization technologies. In China, consumers favor instant messaging on PCs and text messaging on cellular telephones over e-mail. Despite the presence of U.S. heavyweights—such as Microsoft (which launched a Chinese version of MSN Messenger three years ago),

Yahoo, and recently MySpace—Shenzhen-based Tencent is the leader in the Chinese market. Its free messenger, QQ, had a market share of 70% to 80% in 2006, compared with 15% for MSN Messenger, according to Shanghai-based iResearch. QQ's cute penguin mascot and ultrasimple interface endear it to China's internet users, 70% of whom are younger than 30. In addition to the free chat program and chat rooms, QQ offers games, virtual pets, and ringtone downloads.

The U.S. players have tried to capitalize on users' desire to form cybercommunities, but Tencent has taken a different route: It taps into the Chinese craving for freedom of expression. QQ offers digital avatars that users can personalize online, from the clothes they wear to the virtual cars they drive. People can choose from a dizzying array of virtual outfits and accessories, each costing just RMB 1 or 2. The Chinese love the idea of customizing their online messengers, and in less than a decade QQ has become the market leader. "QQ" has even become a verb, and the phrase "QQ me" has been used in pop songs. Since its founding in 1998, Tencent has made steady progress: It had 220 million active users (caveat: many Chinese have more than one online identity) and US$375 million in revenues in 2006—and counting.

Other local winners' customization techniques are simple. The companies package products innovatively to make them affordable. In India's $500 million hair care market, the well-entrenched multinational incumbent Hindustan Unilever, which has operated there since 1933, and challengers such as America's Procter & Gamble and France's L'Oréal have been slugging it out in the cities for decades. While Hindustan Unilever and P&G are the leaders with 36% and 27% of the market in 2006, respectively, according to Datamonitor, CavinKare, a local company, is giving them a run for their money with its market share of 16%. The Chennai-based start-up, established in 1983, packs shampoo in sachets—an idea its founder borrowed from his father, who pioneered the use of these pouches, and his brothers, who first launched shampoo sachets in 1979.

CavinKare's single-use plastic sachets are convenient to use and easy to store, and they minimize product waste because people are not tempted to use more than what they need for one wash. The packaging size makes shampoo affordable for many Indians who don't earn enough money to spend on big bottles and who regard the product as an expensive indulgence. CavinKare went after lower-income city dwellers and rural consumers for the first time. For years, it found the going tough; the company had to demonstrate how shampoo cleans hair better than soap and used trade-ins and discounts to get people to try it. Once CavinKare tasted success, Hindustan Unilever and P&G started to package shampoo in sachets as well. Price matters, though, and CavinKare's relatively cheap Chik brand has allowed the company to become the largest local shampoo player in India.

Develop Business Models to Overcome Key Obstacles

Multinational corporations often complain about insurmountable problems—structural issues such as a lack of distribution channels, or infrastructural hurdles like limited telecommunications bandwidth—that prevent them from doing business in their usual way. Smart local companies are adept at identifying the key challenges that their markets pose and, from the get-go, at designing strategies to overcome or sidestep those obstacles. Sure, multinational enterprises later copy the same tactics, but by then the local ones have sharpened their first-mover advantage.

For instance, the global leaders in video games, such as Microsoft, Nintendo, and Sony, haven't made much headway in China because of software piracy. Does that mean China doesn't have much of a market for games? Of course not. Chinese companies such as Shanda, which entered the industry in 2001, have developed a thriving game business by developing massively multiplayer online role-playing games (MMORPGs) instead. These products are impossible to pirate since they are live experiences created by technologies that link many players over the internet. China's youth, eager for entertainment options, have warmed to the idea. China's MMORPG industry, which generated revenues of about $600 million in 2005, has been growing at 40% a year since 2003, according to iResearch. Belatedly in 2007, Electronic Arts acquired a 15% equity stake in one of Shanda's competitors, The9, for $167 million.

It's tough to make money on the internet in China because of consumer concerns about online theft and the lack of a credit card culture. Shanda has tackled the online-payment problem by taking transactions offline. China's gamers purchase prepaid cards from local merchants. When they scratch the film off the card, they get a number that entitles them to a fixed amount of game-playing time online. Shanda keeps adapting its business model. Sensing that Chinese gamers are becoming less willing to pay to play, it now offers free access to old games. It makes money, as Tencent does, by selling virtual merchandise such as weapons and equipment. The company is also moving into mobile gaming, which is set to take off. Later this year, Shanda will launch mobile versions of its popular *World of Legend* and *Magical Land* role-playing games on customized Motorola handsets.

Innovative strategies sometimes create new businesses in addition to giving local champions an edge. In Mexico, Grupo Elektra wanted to be a successful retailer, but it created a banking business along the way. The company realized early that to make money, it had to sell big-ticket items such as washing machines and refrigerators. Many middle- and low-income Mexicans could buy consumer durables only by taking loans or paying in installments. They couldn't get credit easily because Mexico's commercial banks didn't consider them creditworthy or know how to evaluate their repayment potential. Grupo Elektra started offering consumer financing and, effectively, selling products on installment plans. Once the company offered credit, its business took off. In 1987 Grupo Elektra operated 59 stores; today it runs more than 1,600, making it one of the largest retailers in Mexico. Imitation is a form of followership: Wal-Mart, which is Mexico's largest retailer by sales, obtained a banking license in November 2006 to offer financial services in all its 997 Mexican stores.

In 2002, Grupo Elektra, which still sells about 60% of its goods on credit, set up a full-fledged bank, Banco Azteca, with branches inside Elektra stores. The bank's business, measured by assets under management, has had a compound annual growth rate of 133% for the past five years. Given that most customers have no credit histories, the bank has developed a novel credit-appraisal system. A corps of 4,000 loan officers uses motorcycles to visit prospective borrowers' homes. These officers on wheels assess whether each applicant's standard of living matches the claimed income level and conduct an on-the-spot credit assessment. Collectively, the corps clears as many as 13,000 new loans a day. This unique system has worked so far: Banco Azteca's repayment rate in 2006 was 90%.

Deploy the Latest Technologies

Contrary to popular perceptions, local winners' products and services often incorporate the latest technologies, as the cases of Shanda and Tencent show. New technologies keep operating costs low and enable companies to deliver good-quality products and services. That helps them outperform competitors that believe they can satisfy local consumers with older technologies.

Unburdened by past investments or old processes, younger companies in particular invest in the state of the art to lower costs and offer customers novel features. For example, Brazil's Gol Linhas Aéreas Inteligentes, South America's first low-cost airline, has shaken up the market since it started flying with five aircraft in January 2001. Gol's share of the domestic market, based on revenue passenger-kilometers, grew from 5% in 2001 to 37% in 2006, according to Brazil's civil aviation authority, Agência Nacional de Aviação Civil (ANAC). The world's second-most profitable airline after Ireland's Ryanair, Gol can attribute its success partly to its single-aircraft type of fleet—a model Southwest Airlines pioneered—and to investments in the latest models. In 2007, Gol operated 97 single-class Boeing 737 aircraft, and it had placed orders with Boeing for 64 new 737-800 aircraft that would join the fleet between 2008 and 2010. By buying an aircraft model with a capacity approximately 30% higher than that of its predecessor, Gol will be able to use its landing slots more effectively.

The planes in Gol's fleet were, on average, less than eight years old in December 2006, making it one of the youngest in South America. A young fleet requires less maintenance, so Gol manages quick aircraft turn-arounds and operates more flights per day with each plane. In 2006, Gol's aircraft utilization rate (the time between a plane's departure from the gate and arrival at its destination) was 14.2 block hours a day—the highest in South America, according to ANAC—and the airline boasted the lowest cost per available-seat-kilometer. Gol has also reduced costs by using the latest technology in other operational areas. It was the first Brazilian airline to issue e-tickets and promote internet-based sales; in 2006, it sold 82% of its tickets on its website. Customers can check in on the internet or, if they don't have Web access, there are kiosks and attendants with wireless-enabled pocket PCs to process check-ins. Gol's call centers employ the latest automated voice recognition software to handle high call volumes with a limited staff.

New technologies can help old companies get a second wind after economic liberalization. Gujarat Cooperative Milk Marketing Federation (GCMMF), India's largest dairy company, manufactures and markets a range of dairy products under the brand name Amul. Despite the fierce competition that has come with the opening up of India's dairy industry to big business, the enterprise has managed to stay ahead, in part because it has invested in the latest technologies. For instance, it can collect and process 6.5 million liters of fresh milk every day from close to 13,000 villages in the western state of Gujarat. Farmers bring their milk to collection centers, each located roughly five to 10 kilometers away from a village, twice a day. Thanks to a new milk collection system, GCMMF's field staff can weigh the milk, measure the fat content, and pay the farmer—in less than five minutes. That contrasts with the old system whereby employees took samples and performed fat-content tests days later at a central facility. Not only did farmers have to wait for a week to receive payment, but the lack of transparency led to complaints about fraud.

GCMMF employs satellite communication technologies to collect and track transaction data. A customized ERP system coordinates all the back-office functions and analyzes data in real time to forecast imbalances between the demand for milk products and milk supplies. Its technological infrastructure permits the cooperative to make 10 million error-free payments every day, totaling US$4.3 million (170 million rupees) in cash, and to coordinate large numbers of trucks and processing plants with military precision. That efficiency has enabled GCMMF to penetrate India's urban and rural markets deeply.

Take Advantage of Low-Cost Labor, and Train Staff In-House

Many local champions have at their core a business model that taps a pool of low-cost labor instead of relying on automation. Consider, for instance, Focus Media, which has become China's largest outdoor advertising firm. It has placed LCD displays that it engineered in-house in more than 130,000 locations in 90 cities to create a national advertising platform. The company's screens are in office buildings, apartment blocks, retail stores, shopping malls, restaurants, hospitals, drugstores, beauty salons, health clubs, golf courses, hotels, airports, and airport transit buses.

Focus Media uses a decidedly low-tech solution to refresh and service all those LCD screens: a veritable army of employees who move from building to building on bicycles and replace, whenever necessary, the DVDs and flashcards that play the advertisements. Focus Media could link the LCD screens electronically—as any blue-blooded transnational company would—but it does not. Using people keeps the company's operating costs low while enabling it to offer clients a great deal of flexibility. For a small premium, Focus Media will allow a client to flash ads on office buildings nationwide on the week of a major product launch; or target only outdoor plaza locations on one weekend in one city; or use a mix of online, in-cinema, and shopping-center advertisements the day before Chinese New Year. Were Focus Media to use an automated system, the Chinese government could deem it a network-based broadcaster and regulate it as a media company, which might curtail its growth. Focus Media's bicycle-based solution fits well within an otherwise high-tech business.

At the other end of the labor spectrum, skilled talent is hard to find and difficult to retain in emerging markets. Successful companies such as Grupo Elektra, Gol, China Merchants Bank, and India's ITC invest heavily in in-house training. India's Apollo Hospitals, another case in point, has developed a good reputation by recruiting some of the country's best doctors and nurses. The quality of its services is a key differentiator, allowing the chain to charge patients 10 times what they would pay in a public hospital. Although the company employs 4,000 specialists and 3,000 medical officers at 41 facilities, it needs more people to staff new hospitals and to offer additional services. Recognizing that India's medical education infrastructure is growing slowly, Apollo Hospitals established a foundation in 1998 to finance new teaching institutes, including one that offers a postgraduate degree in hospital management and a nursing school. That's not all. In 2000, Apollo Hospitals and a leading Indian technology training company, NIIT, set up a joint venture to offer online medical classes. Medvarsity Online offers postgraduate courses in family medicine, emergency medicine, and health insurance. Apollo Hospitals has also introduced programs to train physiotherapists, medical technicians, and laboratory technicians. It provides nurses with medical training as well as communication and customer-service skills. Without all these investments in training, Apollo Hospitals would not have been able to sustain its growth.

Scale Up Quickly

In many emerging markets, when a new business opportunity becomes apparent, several companies crop up to capitalize on it. The size of countries like China, India, and Brazil—particularly the large number of provinces and cities—allows regional players to flourish. However, only companies that operate nationwide can reap the benefits of scale. Many homegrown champions go after scale economies after generating economies of scope.

Expansion often entails mergers and acquisitions. Focus Media, for instance, faced many rivals scattered across China's cities when it started out in 2003. It pursued an aggressive acquisition-led strategy, which soon gave it the nationwide reach to attract advertisers and diminish the competitiveness of regional rivals. By scaling up quickly, Focus Media vaulted past two global leaders in China's outdoor-advertising industry: America's Clear Channel Communications and France's JCDecaux. In 2006, Clear Channel was less than half of Focus Media's size in terms of revenue, even though it had set up shop in China back in 1998. JCDecaux, which entered the country by acquiring two companies in 2005, doesn't report its China revenues. However, it operates in only 20 cities, compared with Focus Media's presence in 90. While Clear Channel and JCDecaux have made a few acquisitions in the past decade, Focus

Media struck five deals between January 2006 and February 2007 in order to cement its leadership.

Some local champions create regional entities to speed up organic growth. For example, Goodbaby has set up 35 companies, each operating in a Chinese province or a city, to strike local distribution agreements and to open new points of presence quickly. That has spawned one of the most extensive marketing and sales networks in the country: 1,600 stand-alone stores or department-store counters and 300 distributors. By 2010, the company plans to have opened 500 more locations. In addition, Goodbaby opened the first in a series of flagship stores two years ago. These sites offer a few foreign brands, Goodbaby's own products, and access to professionals who dispense parenting advice. By overcoming the distribution challenges of the Chinese market quickly, Goodbaby has laid the foundation for success.

Invest in Talent to Sustain Rapid Growth

In market after market in emerging economies, invading multinational corporations encounter domestic rivals with the entrepreneurial zeal and the knack to keep growing quickly for a long time. They discover, to their shock, that there are great local managers in these countries. In fact, most transnational giants underestimate the management depth and capability of rivals that have the additional advantage of not needing to negotiate with headquarters in a distant First World city.

Many companies face the risk of meltdown when they grow at double-digit rates for years. There are no silver bullets to prevent that altogether, but smart organizations minimize senior management turnover and institutionalize management systems to tackle the complexities of rapid growth. Consider Russia's Wimm-Bill-Dann Foods (WBD), which five entrepreneurs founded in 1992 with borrowed funds. They leased a production line at the partially idle Lianozovsky Dairy Plant near Moscow to make fruit juices and decided to make a foray into the dairy industry. Since the short shelf life of dairy products limits their distribution to a radius of 400 kilometers, WBD had to manufacture products close to consumers. Between 1995 and 2003, the company acquired 19 dairy companies and created a national distribution system by appointing 100 distributors. However, by 2003, multinational companies such as Danone and Coca-Cola also built strong sales and distribution systems and capitalized on the growth of local retailers to storm the Russian market. Soon, Danone's dairy products and Coca-Cola's fruit juices were selling faster than WBD's products.

The founders of WBD realized that they needed to adopt a new approach in order to retain the company's leadership position. In April 2006, they hired a new CEO, who had worked with Coca-Cola in Europe for 20 years. To allow him a free hand, the founders moved into new roles as members of a supervisory board. They helped create a more powerful corporate center and a new company mission. Led by the new CEO, WBD focused on reducing costs; improving quality; and investing in its people, including executives. To ensure high quality at a reasonable cost, the company drew up detailed specifications for all of its products and raw materials, improved forecasting and demand planning, reengineered processes to eliminate bureaucracy, simplified its legal structure, and invested in information technology. WBD adopted a number of human resource management practices including a key performance indicator system, semiannual performance reviews, and individual development plans for the top 500 employees. It also linked salaries with performance and offered stock options to top managers for the first time. Finally, WBD brought in seasoned managers, many from multinational companies, even as it sought to maintain the culture of a Russian company. Partly as a result, WBD had around 34% of the Russian market for packaged dairy products in 2006, according to ACNielsen—more than double Danone's 16% share—and was one of the top three players in fruit juices, with an 18% share.

Like WBD, many national champions have used the appeal of ballooning equity valuations and the prospect of rapid career advancement to attract talent from multinational companies. Gone are the days when executives regarded working for a foreign corporation as something special; now they believe it is just as rewarding to work for a homegrown giant. Several executives have left multinational companies or jobs abroad to join local leaders. In China, for instance, Focus Media CFO Mingdong Wu used to work for Merrill Lynch; Ctrip chairman Jianzhang Liang is a veteran of Oracle, and CFO Jie Sun used to work for KPMG; and Shanda president Jun Tang previously headed Microsoft's China business, and CFO Yong Zhang came from PricewaterhouseCoopers.

How One Local Winner Wove Its Strategy

Many companies pursue one or the other of the success strategies just described. What distinguishes winners is their ability to pursue several, or often all, of them simultaneously and to execute them well. Ctrip, China's largest travel consolidator and online travel agent, has been able to do just that. Founded in 1999, the start-up recognized at the outset that online travel services such as Travelocity, Orbitz, and Expedia wouldn't do well in China with the business models they use so effectively in the United States. At the time, China didn't have a national ticketing system, such as Sabre, and it still lacks a secure online-payment system. Most of the country's hotels don't belong to a global or national chain, and most local airlines and consumers prefer paper tickets to electronic tickets. Ctrip therefore decided to focus on both off-line and online sales.

Chinese consumers prefer to deal with travel agents, so Ctrip has set up a call center where more than 3,000 representatives can serve 100,000 customers a day. To break into the corporate travel services market, where personal relationships dominate, Ctrip has cleverly developed a loyalty program for executive assistants. Although 70% of Ctrip's revenues still come from off-line sales, it has invested in a sophisticated, automated voice-response system so that it can offer 24/7 booking to consumers. The company has also developed a booking infrastructure that links its online and call center operations to a central database. A large team of researchers constantly updates the database while technical experts integrate it with the systems of Ctrip's airline and hotel partners that are slowly computerizing their operations. The database has yielded the company a formidable advantage since most rivals lack a similar system. In a classic move to use low-cost labor, Ctrip collects payments and provides delivery of paper tickets through couriers who get around China's cities on bicycles and scooters.

It's tough to operate in China's travel market, which comprises hundreds of cities in dozens of provinces, because of regulatory and licensing barriers. Setting up shop in each city requires a license from the local government, which usually owns a competing travel company. There's also the challenge of organizing sales teams and delivery services in many cities. Over the past 10 years, Ctrip has patiently overcome these hurdles and built a national travel business with 5,600 hotel partners and alliances with all of China's leading airlines. Recognizing that Ctrip is a widely dispersed organization, senior executives have created a company-wide management culture, the Ctrip Way, and they emphasize the use of common business processes across the company. Ctrip has even established Six Sigma standards for customer-service operations and expects employees to meet them. Furthermore, the company has a strong management team with its co-founders still at the helm. Not surprisingly, Ctrip has beaten back several foreign competitors, such as Expedia's eLong.com and Travelocity's Zuji.com as well as Travelsky, the online portal launched by Chinese state-owned airlines and foreign investors such as Sabre in 2001. At the time, many believed that Travelsky would be the winner in China since it had government backing and priority access to airline tickets. However, it hasn't caught up with Ctrip, at least not yet.

Beating the Locals at Their Own Game

If multinational companies are to succeed on local champions' home turf, they have to fight on two fronts. First, they must emulate some of the local companies' strategies, as we said earlier. Second, they must develop other strategies that local companies cannot easily copy. That's tough but not impossible, as is clear from the recent experiences in China of three multinational companies, each from a different continent and industry.

Kentucky-based Yum Brands, which owns restaurant chains such as KFC, Pizza Hut, and Taco Bell, is thriving in China. The company has adapted in many ways in order to break into the Chinese market. It has customized menus to local tastes and has launched dozens of new items each year. It has also tailored store formats to consumers' behavior, and as preferences change, it modifies those formats. For example, Yum recently introduced drive-throughs to cater to China's growing car-driving population. Its marketing emphasizes educational content, not just food, so its restaurants appeal to parents' priorities. The company positions stores as fun places; for instance, a KFC outlet in China averages two birthday parties a day. In addition, Yum has grown faster than McDonald's. In 2002, KFC outlets in China numbered 766, compared with 538 for McDonald's; by November 2007, the gap had widened to about 2,000 KFC restaurants (in 420 Chinese cities and towns) versus about 800 McDonald's locations. The company is also expanding Pizza Hut, which has nearly 300 restaurants in China, and its local chain, East Dawning, which serves Chinese food. In fact, Yum opens an average of one new restaurant every day in China.

Yum uses its global expertise to differentiate itself from local players. A network of 16 distribution and two processing centers supports its expansion. To ensure consistent deliveries of quality raw materials, the company has adopted tough supplier-selection policies. Yum also uses its global reputation and resources to influence the Chinese government's policies regarding food safety and supply chain regulations. By doing so, it protects its local reputation, builds government support, and influences industry structure. The result is a combination not easily found in China: a family of quick-service restaurant brands that serve good-quality food in clean environments with local appeal. Yum's strategy is working: Its China business accounted for 20% of its global profits in 2006.

Yum may have set the pace, but Finland's Nokia came from behind to win in China. Five years ago, Nokia trailed Motorola in the Chinese market. It also faced stiff competition from local players such as TCL and Ningbo Bird, whose basic cellular telephones targeted midtier cities and midmarket and low-end customers. In the early 2000s, the local companies moved fast, opening retail outlets and distribution capabilities across China. Surprisingly, Nokia countered equally quickly by investing in a national sales and distribution network. It used a sophisticated IT platform, which provides near real-time information on sales volumes and competitor pricing, as well as an army of 3,000 in-store promoters to push products. Nokia also focused on areas where its Chinese rivals were hard-pressed to match its efforts. For instance, it accelerated product development and launched a stream of innovative cellular telephones. The company rapidly ramped up production of these products to high volumes and leveraged its bargaining power to keep costs competitive. Partly because of these factors, Nokia has become the market leader in China today.

The experience of South Korea's Hyundai shows that even late entrants can succeed in crowded emerging markets. The automaker's share rose from zero in 2002, when it entered China, to 7% in 2006; cumulative sales topped the 500,000 mark just 40 months after launch. Hyundai identified a consumer need that other automakers had overlooked, because it sent teams who spent months learning what Chinese consumers want. The company noticed that foreign players held the top end of the market and local players the bottom end, but no company offered a good-quality car at an affordable price. Understanding that China's new middle class wanted such a car, Hyundai refined the Sonata and Elantra models for that market.

Hyundai was determined to bring its expertise and experience to China. China's laws require foreign automakers to enter into joint ventures with domestic firms. These arrangements often result in local enterprises' taking control. Hyundai retained operational control of its joint venture but created a healthy working relationship with its partner, Beijing Automotive Industry Holding Corporation (BAIC). For instance, it insisted that South Korean employees who worked in China learn Chinese. Hyundai minimized its up-front investment by using BAIC's functional but labor-intensive production line. It has kept costs down by forcing its South Korean suppliers to set up operations in China. Buoyed by its success in China's fiercely competitive market, Hyundai is building a $1 billion manufacturing plant in Beijing, which will start operations in April 2008 and will double the company's production capacity to 600,000 units a year.

Globalization is clearly a double-edged sword. The advantages of being a transnational corporation in emerging markets have declined dramatically in recent times. Smart local companies have used the benefits of globalization to close gaps in technology, capital, and talent with their rivals from the developed world. Although the average local competitor is weak, transnational corporations would do well to rethink their strategies. After all, it often takes only one strong homegrown champion to shut a multinational out of an emerging market.

ARINDAM K. BHATTACHARYA is a Delhi-based partner and managing director, and **DAVID C. MICHAEL** is a Beijing-based senior partner and managing director, of the Boston Consulting Group.

Originally published in March 2008. Reprint R0803F

China + India

The Power of Two
by Tarun Khanna

A HISTORIC EVENT, LARGELY unnoticed by the rest of the world, took place on the border between China and India on July 6, 2006. After 44 years, the Asian neighbors reopened Nathu La, a mountain pass perched 14,140 feet up in the eastern Himalayas, connecting Tibet in China to Sikkim in India. Braving heavy wind and rain, several dignitaries—including China's ambassador to India, the Tibet Autonomous Region's chairperson, and Sikkim's chief minister—watched as soldiers removed a barbed wire fence between the two nations.

Companies all over the world would do well to hear the winds of change roaring through Nathu La (which in Tibetan means "Listening Ears Pass"). The decision to reopen the world's highest customs post marked the culmination of a slow but steady process of rapprochement between China and India. The friends turned foes in 1962, when they fought a short but bloody war. After that, the two nations' armies glared at each other, weapons at the ready, until their governments decided to fight poverty rather than each other. In the past few years, China (under President Hu Jintao and Premier Wen Jiabao) and India (led by Prime Minister Manmohan Singh) have forged links anew. China now supports India's bid for a permanent seat on the United Nations Security Council; their armies have held joint military exercises; and at World Trade Organization negotiations, the countries have adopted similar positions on international trade in agricultural products and intellectual property rights.

The two nations are also reviving their old cultural and religious ties. Beginning in 2012, they will allow tourists to use Nathu La, which will increase the number of cross-border pilgrimages. The pass makes it easy for China's Buddhists to offer prayers at monasteries in Sikkim, such as Rumtek, and for India's Hindus and Jains to visit sacred Mount Kailash and Manasarovar Lake in Tibet. The bonds between China and India run deep. Four out of five Chinese, from a broad cross-section of society, told me in an informal survey that Bollywood movies come immediately to mind when they think about India. That's despite the fact that it has been more than a decade since Indian movies were the only foreign films shown in China. Ignoring these facts would be a mistake; several scholars, such as Baruch College's Tansen Sen, have argued that religion and culture lubricate the wheels of commerce.

China and India are also rebuilding their business bridges. Although Nathu La's reopening may be largely symbolic—the two countries allow the trade of only a

Idea in Brief

China and India are burying the hatchet after four-plus decades of hostility. A few companies from both nations have been quick to gain competitive advantages by viewing the two as symbiotic. If Western corporations fail to do the same, they will lose their competitive edge—and not just in China and India but globally. The trouble is, most companies and consultants refuse to believe that the planet's most populous nations can mend fences. Not only do the neighbors annoy each other with their foreign policies, but they're also vying to dominate Asia. Moreover, the world's fastest-growing economies are archrivals for raw materials, technologies, capital, and overseas markets. Still, China and India are learning to cooperate, for three reasons. First, these ancient civilizations may have been at odds since 1962, but for 2,000 years before that, they enjoyed close economic, cultural, and religious ties. Second, neighbors trade more than non-neighbors do, research suggests. Third, China and India have evolved in very different ways since their economies opened up, reducing the competitiveness between them and enhancing the complementarities. Some companies have already developed strategies that make use of both countries' capabilities. India's Mahindra & Mahindra developed a tractor domestically but manufactures it in China. China's Huawei has recruited 1,500 engineers in India to develop software for its telecommunications products. Even the countries' state-owned oil companies, including Sinopec and ONGC, have teamed up to hunt for oil together. Multinational companies usually find that tapping synergies across countries is difficult. At least two American corporations, GE and Microsoft, have effectively combined their China and India strategies, allowing them to stay ahead of global rivals.

few products, such as raw silk, horses, and tea, across the pass—it indicates a fresh camaraderie between the planet's fastest-growing economies. Their desire to strike a partnership is evident: High-level official visits

India + China

India

- Area: 3,287,590 sq km (2007)
- Population: 1.13 billion (2007)
- GDP real growth rate: 9.4%
- GDP per capita (ppp)*: $3,800
- Unemployment: 7.8% (2006)
- Population below poverty line: 25% (2002)
- Exports: $112 billion
- Imports: $187.9 billion
- Exchange rate: 39.80 rupees per $ (2007)
- Imports from: China, U.S., Germany, Singapore
- Exports to: U.S., UAE, China, UK
- Literacy rate: 61% (2001)
- Life expectancy: 68.59 years (2007)

*purchasing power parity

China

- Area: 9,596,960 sq km (2007)
- Population: 1.32 billion (2007)
- GDP real growth rate: 11.1%
- GDP per capita (ppp)*: $7,800
- Unemployment: 4.2% (2005)
- Population below poverty line: 10% (2004)
- Exports: $974 billion
- Imports: $777.9 billion
- Exchange rate: 7.52 RMB per $ (2007)
- Imports from: Japan, S. Korea, U.S., Germany
- Exports to: U.S., Japan, S. Korea, Germany
- Literacy rate: 90.9% (2000)
- Life expectancy: 72.88 years (2007)

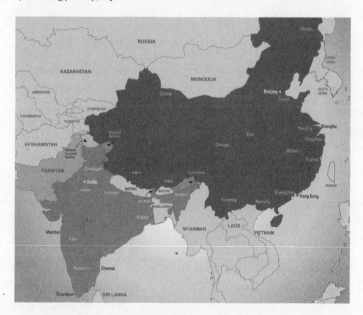

Sources: CIA World Factbook; www.xe.com. Data are based on 2006 estimates, except where otherwise specified.

often take place between them; businesspeople from each country participate in conferences held in the other; and forecasts of the flow of goods and services between them keep rising. Sino-Indian trade stagnated at around $250 million a year in the 1990s, but it touched $13 billion in 2006, will cross the $20 billion mark in 2007, and may exceed $30 billion in 2008—a growth rate of more than 50% a year.

Yet most enterprises and experts gloss over this budding business axis. I hear the naysayers all the time. China and India can't collaborate; they can only compete, say many Western (and not a few Chinese and Indian) academics and consultants. Both nations are vying to be Asia's undisputed superpower, and they are suspicious about each other's intentions. China and India have nuclear weapons; they have created the world's biggest armies; and they are trying to dominate the seas in the region. China continues to support Pakistan, which India isn't happy about, and India still lets in Tibetan refugees, which China resents. The United States, meanwhile, plays India against China. In addition, since most adult Chinese and Indians grew up seeing each other as aggressors, it's tough for them to trust each other.

Moreover, the argument runs, China and India are business rivals at heart. The former's remarkable economic rise threatens India, which trails its neighbor on almost every conventional socioeconomic indicator. China may be strong in manufacturing and infrastructure and India in services and information technology, but the latter's manufacturing industry is becoming globally competitive, while China's technology sector threatens to match India's in a decade. Both have a growing appetite for natural resources such as oil, coal, and iron ore, for which they compete fiercely. They also fight for capital, especially for investments by multinational companies from North America, Europe, and Japan. All this makes it difficult to believe that China and India can ever cooperate. Few people think to ask, "Can China and India work together?" Instead, a big question debated in boardrooms is whether India can catch up with China.

This perspective is incomplete. China is home to 1.3 billion people; India has a population of 1.1 billion. In the next decade, they will become the largest and third-largest economies in terms of purchasing power. By 2016 they will account for around 40% of world trade, compared with 15% in 2006. That's roughly the position they occupied about 200 years ago. Economist Angus Maddison has calculated that in the 1800s, China and India together accounted for 50% of global trade. It is impossible to make predictions about the integration of these countries into the global economy, because past events, such as Germany's reunification and the fall of the Iron Curtain, don't compare. After those occurrences in 1990, a large number of people entered the global economy, but the numbers pale in significance when compared with the China–India double whammy. Like it or not, the world's future is tied to China and India.

Both countries have put feeding their millions ahead of border disputes, and they can't turn the clock back on liberalization. They have too much to lose by not working together. This doesn't suggest that a lovefest will ensue; it only implies less hostility and suspicion between two fast-maturing nations.

China and India have taken different routes to enter the world economy, and that has resulted in their gaining complementary strengths. Some business leaders have learned to make use of both countries' resources and capabilities, as I shall show in the following pages. In the process, they have become globally competitive. Multinational companies will only lose if they don't take advantage of the complementarities between the two economies. If they embrace both countries, however, they can tap into diverse strengths almost as easily as Chinese and Indian companies will.

Fathoming the Depth of Their Relationship

The tensions between China and India are real, but they will eventually prove to be aberrant. There are three good reasons for believing that: one historic, one economic, and one strategic.

First, China and India sealed their borders in modern times, but in the 2,000 years preceding the conflict of 1962, the two countries enjoyed strong economic, religious, and cultural ties. By the second century BC, the southern branch of the Silk Road—an interconnected series of ancient trade routes on land and sea—linked the cities of Xi'an in China and Pataliputra in India. Trade on the Tea and Horse Road, as the Chinese called it, was a significant factor in the growth of the Chinese

---

How China and India have developed differently

China and India are large, populous Asian neighbors, but the similarities end there. The differences between them make the whole greater than the sum of the parts.

	China	India
Foundations	**Government** A single party rules China. Those at the top control the reforms process, although bureaucrats located far from Beijing don't always do its bidding. Officials who deliver economic growth can move up the ladder.	**Government** Coalitions of political parties jockey for power in a raucous democracy. Positions of power aren't dominated by traditional economic or social elites. Individual rights are respected, but the presence of many interest groups often renders the system dysfunctional.
	Information and transparency Economic information is increasingly available, but political information is not. The state's efforts to curtail news compete with technology-based efforts to disseminate information.	**Information and transparency** There's a cacophony of voices that are rarely deliberately inaccurate. The media debate everything; nothing is off-limits. In fact, they are increasingly exposing corruption in high places.
	Property rights The state respects the individual's rights to property more than it used to, but it still sacrifices them on the altar of public interest when the two come in conflict. The state can therefore make huge investments in public goods.	**Property rights** The individual's rights to property are sacrosanct. Public interest is often sacrificed for the individual's sake. The government can make only small investments in public goods, which has led to poor infrastructure.
Implications	**Local business** The country has millions of would-be entrepreneurs, but their potential is constrained unless they partner with the state or with foreigners. The government is often the entrepreneur.	**Local business** Indigenous enterprise has flowered in the past 15 years. It is aided by effective capital markets, good information flows, and respect for property rights.

and Indian civilizations. Seen in that light, the closing of the Sino–Indian border—not the border's reopening—is the anomaly.

Implications	**Multinational companies** Foreign companies get red-carpet treatment from the state. Since they usually rely on their home bases for capital and senior talent, they aren't affected much by China's poor markets.	**Multinational companies** The government continues to exhibit a distaste for foreign investment, although less so than in the past. That's partly for good reasons, like supporting indigenous entrepreneurs, and partly for bad ones, such as protectionism.
	Diaspora Overseas Chinese played a catalytic role in starting China's economic miracle two decades ago. They are still a source of capital, while Chinese returning home contribute brainpower.	**Diaspora** Once shunned, nonresident Indians are more accepted than they used to be. Capital flows from overseas Indians come in the form of remittances, not investments.
	Rural economy The physical infrastructure in the villages is often superb. But the relative decline in the rural standard of living, compared with that in coastal areas, has fueled protest and resentment.	**Rural economy** The state's utter neglect of rural India has left villagers impoverished. The infrastructure is usually in terrible shape. The efforts made by the private sector and civil society to help villagers are laudable but inadequate.
	Education and health The resource-rich state has made large investments in education. Basic literacy levels are very high. The quality of health care is bad, partly because China moved away from a centralized system to a private model after 1978.	**Education and health** The state has made woefully inadequate investments in education. The quality of health care, especially for the masses, is terrible. Private-sector investments help compensate, but they aren't large enough to make an impact.
	External relations A flat-driven approach characterizes China's relations with the world. The country leads with its wallet. China is stronger than India in their common hinterland in Asia and is gaining prominence in Africa and central Asia.	**External relations** The state's inefficiency extends to projecting India's influence. India's best brand ambassadors are its companies, executives, academics, and film stars. India is incapable of using hard power but is a masterful exponent of soft power.

In fact, Buddhism traveled from India to China in 67 AD along the Silk Road. In those days, the relationship between China and India was one of mutual respect and admiration. The monk Fa-hsien (337 to 422 AD), who traveled from China to India to study Buddhism, referred to the latter as *Madhyadesa* (Sanskrit for "Middle Kingdom"), which is similar in meaning to *Zhongguo,* the word the Chinese used to describe China. In the 1930s, no less a scholar than Beijing University's Hu Shih said that the sixth century AD marked the "Indianization of China." Even today, visits by Chinese and Indian leaders include a trip to a Buddhist shrine in the host nation.

There was also much goodwill after the birth of the two modern states, India in 1947 and China in 1949. During the 1930s, India's future prime minister Jawaharlal Nehru frequently wrote about how India supported the struggles of fellow Asians under the foreign yoke. He organized marches in India in support of China's freedom, organized a boycott of Japanese goods, and in 1937 sent a medical mission to help the Chinese. India was the second non-Communist country, after Burma, to recognize the People's Republic of China, in 1950. Five years later, India supported the idea that China should attend the Bandung Conference, in Indonesia, which led to the creation of the Non-Aligned Movement, an alliance of developing countries that supported neither the United States nor the Soviet Union. In those heady years, one slogan heard in India was *Hindi Chini Bhai Bhai* ("Indians and Chinese are Brothers"). The slogan hasn't been forgotten; China's premier, Wen Jiabao, repeated it in 2006 when he visited the Indian Institute of Technology in Delhi.

Second, economists tell us that neighbors tend to trade more than other nations do. An official committee set up to encourage commerce between China and India recently suggested that bilateral trade could touch $50 billion by 2010. Even the official numbers understate the potential, according to economists who use gravity models to estimate what the trade between two countries should be. Such models calculate potential bilateral trade as a function of the size of the nations, the physical distance between them, and other factors such as whether they share a language, a colonial past, a border, membership of a free-trade zone, and so on. Sino-Indian trade today is up to 40% less than it could be, according to those models. Moreover, Sino-Indian trade is more balanced than China's trade with the United States and Europe; the latter countries' large deficits cause political friction.

Third, China and India, after they cut themselves off from each other, evolved in complementary ways that reduced the competitiveness between them. What China is good at, India is not—and vice versa. China instituted sweeping economic reforms in 1978 and has steadily opened up thereafter. A balance-of-payments crisis forced India's reforms in 1991, but because of political factors, liberalization has been slow and piecemeal there ever since. China uses top-down authority to channel entrepreneurship; in fact, the government is the entrepreneur in many cases. India revels in a private sector-led frenzy, and its government is incapable of efficiency. China struggles to control fixed asset investment, while India is constrained by scarce capital. China welcomes foreigners, shunning only those who are not part of its power structure. India shuns foreigners and mollycoddles its own. China's capital markets are non-existent; India's are among the best in the emerging markets. And so on. There are no two countries more yin and yang than China and India.

As a result, the kinds of companies that flourish in China and India are very different. As my HBS colleague Krishna Palepu and I argued in an earlier HBR article ("Emerging Giants: Building World-Class Companies in Developing Countries," October 2006), companies are usually reflections of the institutional contexts in their home countries. In China, where protection of intellectual property rights is nascent and the government curtails some forms of expression, entrepreneurs don't push the creative envelope. Instead, it makes sense for them to build manufacturing plants that leverage the superb infrastructure. In India, companies that depend on highway systems and reliable power find it hard to thrive. Those that train and deploy tens of thousands of technically sophisticated, English-speaking university graduates, in contrast, flourish. Both China and India are witnessing an explosion of entrepreneurship, but in ways that make their companies more complementary than the world realizes.

Getting the Best of Both Worlds

These complementarities pose both an opportunity and a threat. It's easy to spot the advantages of treating China and India synergistically and getting the best of both worlds. Companies can use China to make almost anything cheaply. They can turn to India to design and develop products cost-effectively; they can also hire Indian talent to market and service products. For instance, China's Lenovo, which purchased IBM's PC business in 2005, recently moved its global ad-management function from Shanghai to Bangalore. That's because India has a highly creative and sophisticated advertising industry.

To be sure, Chinese and Indian companies will compete intensely with each other. That doesn't mean that the rise of one will necessarily be at the expense of the other. For instance, as the Chinese government tries to develop a software industry, Indian companies such as Infosys, Tata Consultancy Services, and Satyam have been among the first to recruit Chinese engineers. Does that mean they are sowing the seeds of their own destruction? Not really. Most Indian companies have gone into China to provide software services to their multinational clients. Chinese firms will try to compete for those contracts, even as Indian companies fight for a share of the local Chinese market. China will gain from having a software industry, but the benefits may not come at the expense of India's software industry.

The coming together of China and India puts at a disadvantage many companies, especially from the West, that refuse to react to this trend. They will not be able to generate the synergies that their Chinese and Indian rivals can. If they lose share in those two markets, they are—given China's and India's size—unlikely to remain market leaders for very long. Thus, Sino–Indian emerging giants pose a stiffer threat to multinational incumbents than the latter have so far assumed.

Cooperating with Each Other

Already, some Chinese and Indian companies are beginning to view the two countries symbiotically. They are driven not by political factors but by hardheaded self-interest.

India Comes to China

Three years ago, Mahindra & Mahindra, the Indian tractor and automobile maker, reckoned that it would be cheaper to manufacture tractors in China than in India. Besides, the Indian company could gain access to the fast-growing Chinese market only by producing tractors locally. M&M set up a joint venture, Mahindra (China) Tractor, with the Nanchang city government. The partners could not be more different: M&M is a private company led by the third-generation scion of an Indian business family—a far cry from the Chinese government. The Sino–Indian entity purchased Jiangling Tractor, whose plant is located halfway between Shanghai and Guangzhou and has a production capacity of 8,000 tractors per annum.

M&M's low-powered tractors are ideal to till India's fragmented farmland. In 2006 the company held a 30% share of the Indian market, while its closest rival had a 23% share. These tractors also suit China, where the size of the average landholding is now akin to India's. When China's communes broke up and the number of farmers mushroomed, the demand for tractors boomed. The Chinese government also offered financial incentives so farmers would switch from power tillers to tractors, which would reduce the demand for petrol. M&M entered the Chinese market with Jiangling Tractor's Feng-Shou brand. The company has cleverly designed and engineered the model at its facilities in India, while its Chinese company manufactures it.

Mahindra (China) Tractor makes the compact Feng-Shou tractors in the 18-to-35 horsepower (hp) range for the Chinese and foreign markets. It also imports M&M's more powerful 45 hp to 70 hp tractors from India and sells them in China. In February 2005, when I spoke to Anand Mahindra, M&M's CEO, he had nothing but praise for the Chinese company. "We are breaking the myth that it is hard to make money in China or that cultural assimilation is difficult," he told me. "The local disco in Nanchang now plays *bhangra* (a genre of Indian folk music), and the ex-chairman of the Chinese company sang songs from Indian movies at our first banquet." Mahindra said that he had faced no problems in getting Chinese and Indian executives to work together. M&M has posted 15 Indians to the Chinese facility, all of whom report to Chinese supervisors. According to Mahindra, the Indians are none the worse for the experience.

That's not all. M&M realized that it could enter some niche markets in the United States. Many baby boomers have retired from stressful urban lives to places like Flagstaff, Arizona, where for the price of a San Francisco apartment they have bought several acres of land. These hobby farmers need only a small tractor to till the soil. From 2000 to 2005, M&M wrested a 6% share of the U.S. under-70 hp tractor market from companies such as John Deere, New Holland, Agco, and Kubota Tractor. In some southern states such as Texas, M&M's market share is as high as 20%. M&M is giving John Deere in particular a run for its money. In 2004 a Deere dealer advertisement promised a $1,500 rebate to every consumer who traded an M&M for a John Deere. According to M&M executives, when they tracked down tractor owners who had seen the ad, 97% said that they were satisfied with their Made in China and India tractors and did not go for the rebate.

China Comes to India

Just as Mahindra & Mahindra is using China's hard infrastructure, China's Huawei is leveraging India's soft infrastructure to sustain its global edge against Western giants like Cisco. In 1999 the Chinese telecommunications equipment manufacturer set up an Indian company that currently employs around 1,500 engineers. This facility, which is based in Bangalore, develops software solutions in areas such as data communications, network management, operations support systems, and intelligent networks. In 2006 the company opened a second facility in Bangalore, where 180 software engineers develop optical network products and wireless local-area-network solutions.

Huawei has announced that it will invest an additional $100 million to create a single 25-acre campus in Bangalore for 2,000 people. This will enable Huawei India to enter new areas such as optical-transmission networking and sharpen its focus on third-generation networking. While Huawei's development center in

Shenzhen is its most important facility, the Bangalore center (which accounts for about 7% of the company's R&D efforts) is emerging as the second most important. That's partly because of its capabilities. In August 2003, the Indian facility earned the coveted Capability Maturity Model Level 5 certification—the highest quality level for software producers.

Huawei's strategy is noteworthy because India's bureaucracy and polity did everything it could to prevent the company from setting up base. The company persisted, realizing that employing engineers, rather than outsourcing software development to Indian companies, would give it better footing. Jack Lu, who oversees human resources, headed the Bangalore office for three years after setting it up. He says that the main challenge is to overcome each country's stereotypes of the other. For instance, the Indian media portray the Chinese as opportunists set on stealing India's security, software, and telecommunication secrets, and vice versa.

State-Owned Companies Cooperate

Public-sector corporations, the direct arms of two supposedly hostile governments, are also learning to work together. China and India are incredibly energy-deficient, with China importing almost 50% of its oil needs and India more than 70%. Energy companies in both nations have made it a priority to search for "equity" oil. They invest in several countries' petroleum industries to protect themselves against the possibility that one day, political instability in the Middle East will choke off their supplies. This strategy turned

China and India into intense rivals in the international energy industry. Between January and October 2005, China's Sinopec and China National Petroleum Corporation (CNPC) and India's Oil and Natural Gas Corporation (ONGC) clashed over purchases of oil assets in Angola, Ecuador, Kazakhstan, Myanmar, Nigeria, and Russia. Although the Chinese companies won several contracts, they paid more because of the Indian company's aggressive bidding.

In April 2005, Wen Jiabao suggested that China and India think about cooperating in the energy sector. After several meetings of executives from the countries' oil companies, the Chinese and Indian governments signed an agreement in January 2006 about working together on bids for energy resources, and the oil companies signed memorandums of understanding. Incidentally, China teamed up with India partly because it hoped that its companies would get preferential treatment when they bid for infrastructure-related contracts in India.

The Sino–Indian oil hunt has delivered results. In December 2005, CNPC and ONGC won a bid for a 37% stake in Syria's Al Furat Petroleum. Another joint venture between Sinopec and ONGC won a 50% stake in the Colombian oil company Omimex de Colombia in August 2006. In April 2007, ONGC and CNPC agreed to team up to acquire oil assets in Angola and Venezuela. They may also offer each other stakes in other companies they have invested in. Thus, enterprises that everyone thought would bid up the prices of oil assets dramatically are working together in the best interests of China and India.

Viewing the Two as One

It's not surprising that multinational companies find it tough to develop a joint strategy for China and India. Three years ago, I studied the Chinese and Indian sub- sidiaries of 20 Asian companies such as Japan's Asahi Glass, Hitachi, Honda, Mitsui, and Toshiba; South Korea's Samsung, Hyundai, and LG Electronics; and Singapore's DBS Bank and Singapore Telecommunications. Many had operations in both countries, although I included some enterprises that operated in only one of them.

These companies have customized their business models to the local institutional context, which makes it tough for them to generate synergies from their sub- sidiaries in the two countries. For instance, the Chinese subsidiaries are less transparent than the Indian ones be- cause capital allocation does not occur through the finan- cial markets in the former as it does in the latter. The opacity has made it harder for Indian subsidiaries to col- laborate with their Chinese counterparts. The Indian ven- tures also depend on local suppliers more than the Chinese ones do, since they have operated for 39 years, on average, in India and only 18 years in China, having been forced out of the country in the aftermath of the Cul- tural Revolution. However, even in corporations that have entered both countries in the past five years, the re- liance on local suppliers is 60% in India and 10% in China. Thus, the Chinese and Indian subsidiaries use different business models and generate few synergies. Moreover, 31 of the 33 Chinese subsidiaries I studied viewed them- selves as independent of their Indian counterparts, which precluded the chances of cooperation. Relatively few China and India country managers report through their hierarchies to a common decision maker, and companies reward them on the basis of their performance in each country. These organizational factors make it almost impossible for companies to identify opportunities in both China and India that would benefit their strategies.

A final barrier to developing a China–India strategy arises from success. For instance, at Motorola, one of the most successful investors in China, it's easy to imagine a hotline snaking from the China headquarters to Schaumburg, Illinois. Because Motorola has not focused on India nearly as long, that market is starved for attention. The converse is true of Unilever. The company's success in India means that the Indian subsidiary has a direct line to London and Rotterdam, while the China operation doesn't enjoy the same privileges. China shines in Motorola's world; India sparkles in Unilever's. The companies have neglected one of the two markets— and both have achieved less than they could have.

Succeeding from the Outside

It may be difficult for multinational companies to make the best use of China and India, but it isn't impossible. In fact, as GE and Microsoft show, you can skin the proverbial cat in many ways.

GE's Approach
The simplest, and most powerful, way of combining China and India is to focus on hardware in China and on

software in India. As is now well known, that's exactly what GE Healthcare does. For instance, it developed the 719 parts of a high-end Proteus radiology system in a dozen countries. It created the software algorithms and the scanner's generator in Bangalore and allocated part of the hardware manufacturing and assembly to Beijing. The ability to set up parallel groups of highly skilled engineering talent in both countries raises the efficiency of product development and fits in with GE's competitive culture, a senior executive told me.

It's tempting to attribute GE's success to a well-run country manager system. But most companies have similar matrix structures, so that is not the full story. GE did well in China and India because it tailored its business model to the realities of each market. Its early forays into China and India didn't work: GE's business units were unable to profitably sell or develop products locally. Nor could they produce the equipment in other countries at a low enough cost to cater to the low-income populations in the two markets. Experimentation led GE to develop in China and in India parts of what it needed. That process also allowed the company to find ways in which the two subsidiaries could work together. Chinese managers in GE felt that it was in their interest to collaborate with their Indian counterparts, and vice versa. This process took the better part of two decades to come to fruition.

GE also succeeded because it became a good corporate citizen in both countries. Its aircraft engines business has transferred several technologies to China, and its medical diagnostics business is engaged in the debate about health care there. In India, GE was one of the pioneers of business process outsourcing, the practice that put the country on the world's business map. In a vote of confidence in both countries, GE has opened cutting-edge R&D centers in Shanghai and Bangalore. In both China and India, several companies owe their existence to GE. Some were set up by former GE executives; others became world-class by supplying raw materials or components to GE.

Microsoft's Approach

While GE has split the value chain between China and India, Microsoft takes a different tack. It develops innovations that are best suited to China and India respectively.

For example, the company decided to develop mobile-phone-based computing in China, since the country had more than 450 million cellular telephones in 2006 and only 120 million PCs. India had a smaller base of only 166 million mobile phones in 2006. Microsoft created a mobile phone that doubles as a computer when the user attaches it to a device mounted on the side of a TV. You can access the device, FonePlus, with a keyboard, and use the TV screen as a PC monitor. If this experiment succeeds in China, Microsoft will find ways of using FonePlus globally.

In India, Microsoft conducted experiments that would have been much harder to pull off in China. In 2004 the company launched the Windows XP Starter Edition at $25–$30 apiece in India, compared with the pricey full-functionality product. Microsoft decided not to launch the Starter Edition in China, where the top four PC manufacturers control close to two-thirds of the market. The local companies were reluctant to push a low-priced product, since they earn more from the higher-priced version. Because Indian consumers didn't buy the full-functionality Windows, the risks of offering the Starter Edition there were lower than in China. Microsoft's trials in India suggest that the Starter Edition either targets first-time users or induces nonadopters to try out the full-functionality product, so Microsoft China might be willing to market it in the future.

At the same time, Microsoft's China subsidiary is trying to leverage India by forming a three-way venture with the Chinese government and India's largest software company, Tata Consultancy Services (TCS). After entering China in 2002 by setting up a fully owned enterprise in the Hangzhou Special Economic Zone, TCS received the go-ahead in 2007 to expand its presence there. The National Development and Reform Commission authorized the technology parks in Shenzhen and Beijing to buy into TCS's Chinese operations. Incidentally, TCS has gone through three phases in China: It entered China because its global clients were setting up shop there; it then used the country as a base to cater to Asian companies; and, finally, TCS is now going after the Chinese market.

Meanwhile, Microsoft is trying to help the Chinese government build a globally competitive software industry. In keeping with that strategy, Microsoft plans to buy a stake in TCS China, creating an entity that will be 65% owned by TCS, 25% owned by the Chinese software parks, and 10% owned by Microsoft. The Chinese government likes this idea because Microsoft's technologies will spread along with those of TCS. The new venture will develop banking applications for the Beijing and Tianjin city governments. TCS will develop the applications, and Microsoft will use its 17 centers across China to roll them out to the banks. The largest banking applications project TCS has so far undertaken is at the State Bank of India, which has 10,000 branches and 100 million accounts, compared with Bank of China's 22,000 branches and 360 million accounts. That's one more reason China and India are often relevant to each other; no other country has such sprawling networks. It's likely that TCS and Microsoft will one day apply in India the experience they gain in China.

To ensure that China and India don't lack attention, Microsoft has elevated the two country heads to the rank of corporate vice president. They report directly to the person who oversees Microsoft's international operations. They meet frequently to learn from each other. Since there are laboratories and development centers in Beijing and Hyderabad, the heads of R&D in China and India both report to the head of Microsoft's worldwide R&D. The company has also extended the scope of its Redmond, Washington–based Unlimited Potential division, which seeks to bring computer skills and jobs to communities that don't already have them. The division looks at how products that Chinese consumers are using can be sold in India and vice versa, and looks at products that can be sold in other emerging markets worldwide.

It is strange that many people perceive the rise of China and India only as a threat. The idea that these countries' ascent is a zero-sum game—it can occur only at everyone else's expense—defies economic logic. For instance, the United States' job losses in recent times as companies relocated manufacturing facilities and services to China and India are smaller than the unemployment in past decades attributable to structural changes in the U.S. economy. Instead of balking at the inevitable expansion of economic power beyond New York and London, companies will do well to recognize the complementarities between Beijing and New Delhi and, in a fast-changing world, try to wrest competitive advantage from them.

TARUN KHANNA is the Jorge Paulo Lemann Professor at Harvard Business School. This article is adapted in part from his book *Billions of Entrepreneurs: How China and India Are Reshaping Their Futures and Yours* (Harvard Business Review Press, 2008).

Originally published in December 2007. Reprint R0712D

The Battle for Female Talent in Emerging Markets

by Sylvia Ann Hewlett and Ripa Rashid

AFTER WORKING FOR ALMOST 20 years outside China at a global consulting firm, a woman we'll call Mei was recently forced to return home to Beijing, where she faces work/life pressures unrelated to raising children. Mei's elders needed care, and in China a social stigma is attached to using professional help or placing parents in assisted-living facilities. Mei worries about how these obligations will affect her career. Apart from facilitating her return home, however, the firm seems to be unaware of Mei's problems.

In the United Arab Emirates a rising star we'll call Rana is an analyst in the fixed-income division of a bank. Her company regularly offers opportunities for professional development, but Rana had to decline an invitation to a recent training session in New York, because a single woman from the UAE can't board a plane or stay in a hotel unless a male relative is willing to tag along. Adding insult to injury, no video hookup was provided to allow Rana to participate from home.

In many emerging markets, workplace bias seems to escalate for young mothers, who are under constant scrutiny. In India these women commonly return to less-challenging roles or projects or get lower performance ratings. A Brazilian woman told us about a colleague who was fired after being overheard mentioning plans to have a second child. Such explicitly discriminatory behaviors, although they violate company policies, continue unchecked.

Women in these countries face unique challenges, as the stories above show. This presents a major problem for multinational companies whose hopes for growth are pinned on emerging markets. They face a cutthroat war for talent, despite the enormous labor forces of the BRIC countries. India produces as many young engineers as the United States, and Russia produces 10 times as many finance and accounting professionals as Germany. Yet according to the McKinsey Global Institute, a mere 25% of those professionals in India and 20% in Russia are suitable for employment by multinationals. In China less than a 10th of university graduates are prepared to succeed in those organizations.

To meet the talent shortage in emerging markets, multinationals often send managers overseas (not a sustainable solution) or compete with local companies. They need to develop the best-educated and best-prepared managers in those markets, which increasingly means women. Every year large numbers of college-educated

Idea in Brief

Multinational companies are pinning their hopes for growth on emerging markets, specifically in the BRIC countries—Brazil, Russia, India, and China, which together account for 15%-20% of today's global economy. But these companies face a critical obstacle: a cutthroat war for talent. Despite the enormous labor forces in BRIC, top-notch talent is hard to find. India produces as many young engineers as the United States, but according to the McKinsey Global Institute, only 25% of them are suitable for employment by multinationals. Fewer than one out of 10 university graduates in China are prepared to succeed in a multinational environment. To better understand the talent dynamics in emerging markets and how multinational companies can succeed there, the authors launched a study of 4,350 college-educated men and women in Brazil, Russia, India, China, and the United Arab Emirates. They found that the talent solution is in plain sight: Millions of educated women have entered the professional workforce in these countries over the past two decades. Though this talent pool is currently neglected and underleveraged, it represents the future. Women in emerging markets are enormously ambitious and passionate about their work, but they face complicated challenges that are fundamentally different from those of women in the developed world. Here's what companies like Google, Siemens, Intel, GE, and Pfizer are doing to shape talent models that work, especially for women in emerging markets.

women enter the BRIC professional workforce; in 2006 the number was around 26 million. Furthermore, these women are highly ambitious. As we will show, smart multinationals recognize their potential and have found ways to recruit and retain them, giving them the support they need to break through a very thick glass ceiling.

The Talent

To bring these practices to light, we launched a study (the first of its kind) of talent in emerging economies. The study was spearheaded by five global companies that are grappling with the complex challenges associated with globalization: Bloomberg, Booz & Company, Intel, Pfizer, and Siemens. We collected data on 4,350 college-educated men and women in Brazil, Russia, India, China, and the United Arab Emirates, and supplemented them with qualitative research from focus groups, virtual strategy sessions, and interviews with hundreds of white-collar women. Western media often focus on stereotypical images of deprived and oppressed women in less-developed countries, overlooking this vibrant and growing segment of the population. We found that talented women in emerging markets are ahead of the curve in unexpected ways.

Education

Our most surprising finding is that women are flooding into universities and graduate schools: They represent 65% of college graduates in the UAE, 60% in Brazil, and 47% in China. In Russia, where communism promoted universal access to education, 86% of women aged 18 to 23 are enrolled in tertiary education. More than a third in that age group are enrolled in tertiary education in Brazil and the UAE, and 50% of the Indian women (versus 40% of the Indian men) in our sample hold graduate degrees.

Ambition

Although highly educated women the world over are ambitious, the degree of ambition and aspiration among BRIC and UAE women is extraordinary: 85% in India and 92% in the UAE consider themselves very ambitious, and in Russia and China the figures are 63% and 65%, respectively. (Only 36% of U.S. women consider themselves very ambitious.) Furthermore, 80% or more of women in Brazil, India, and the UAE aspire to hold a top job.

Commitment

More than 80% of respondents in Brazil, Russia, India, and the UAE report loving their work, and a similarly high percentage are "willing to go the extra mile" for their companies. This is good news for employers,

Women with ambition

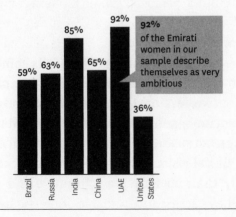

92% of the Emirati women in our sample describe themselves as very ambitious

particularly in light of a 2007–2008 Towers Perrin finding that a mere 21% of global workers are engaged in their work. BRIC and UAE women express a deep connection to and passion for their jobs, citing intellectual stimulation, a sense of personal growth, and the quality of colleagues as key motivators—on a par with job security and compensation. Underlying these factors is the satisfaction of being part of the emerging-market success story. As Leila Hoteit, a UAE-based principal at Booz & Company, puts it, "We have the opportunity to be involved in high impact projects that are reshaping countries and the region as a whole."

The Problem

Unfortunately, female talent is underleveraged in emerging markets. Part of the reason is that family-related pulls and work-related pushes conspire to force women to either settle for dead-end jobs or leave the workforce. The inducements to languish or leave reflect both entrenched cultural perspectives and modern complexities.

Elder Care
As we saw with Mei, family rooted pulls come from a direction that companies might not expect: the older generation. Professional women in BRIC and the UAE are less encumbered than women elsewhere by childcare issues, because many grandparents are active caregivers (cultural visions of old-age pursuits center more on family than on individual leisure), and working mothers have access to affordable domestic help and a

---

Women's income

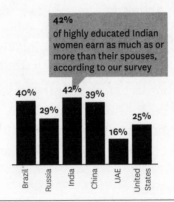

42%
of highly educated Indian women earn as much as or more than their spouses, according to our survey

40%   42% 39%
29%   16% 25%

Brazil · Russia · India · China · UAE · United States

---

growing infrastructure of day-care and early-childhood centers. But in India and China notions of filial piety underpin the cultural value system; although many women in our sample had no children, 70% or more had elder-care responsibilities. In some countries daughterly guilt—and its alternative, daughterly responsibility— are an even greater burden than maternal guilt.

Far more adult women in BRIC and the UAE than in the U.S. live with their parents or in-laws. From 40% to 68% also assist their parents financially, providing 18% to 23% of their elders' income—necessary in countries where state benefits for the elderly are limited or nonexistent. As a highly qualified Emirati woman explained to us, "It is part of the expectation of what children do in the Arab world. We take care of our parents when we grow up."

The Lure of the Public Sector

Family-friendly jobs in the public sector are another oft-ignored pull. More than half our respondents in Brazil, India, and China consider the public sector "very desirable," citing job security, professional opportunities, benefits, and prestige. In the UAE public-sector salaries are equal to or higher than private-sector ones, so Emiratis account for less than 1% of private-sector staff but 54% of employees in federal ministries. A recent Indian study of men and women students found that 60% aspire to public-sector positions over private-sector ones.

Powerful Gender Bias

In BRIC and the UAE professional women face a triple whammy of gender, ethnicity, and cultural attitudes. Of our respondents in Brazil, China, and the UAE, 25% to 36% believe that women are treated unfairly in the workplace because of their gender; in India the number is 45%. In Russia the figure is only 19%, again owing to its communist legacy.

Travel and Safety

Social disapproval of women traveling alone is strong in many societies, with more than half our survey respondents in India and China citing difficulties. This puts industries and corporate positions that require travel at a disadvantage in attracting and retaining talented women. Sales roles in India's pharmaceutical sector, for example, involve frequent trips to semiurban and rural locations, so recruiting women for them is a challenge. The same is true in the industrial and infrastructure

---

Perceived gender discrimination

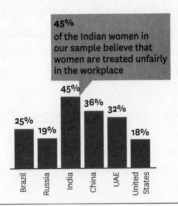

45%
of the Indian women in our sample believe that women are treated unfairly in the workplace

| Brazil | Russia | India | China | UAE | United States |
| 25% | 19% | 45% | 36% | 32% | 18% |

---

sectors. Women often concentrate on careers with local responsibilities—such as medicine, law, hotel administration, advertising, public relations, nursing, and education—or gravitate toward finance and the media, which are city-based and require minimal travel. But even an urban context can be daunting for women. Economic shifts aside, mass culture in India remains tradition-bound and male-dominated. In 2009 commuter trains exclusively for female passengers—Ladies Specials—were introduced in Mumbai, New Delhi, Chennai, and Calcutta to provide a safe haven from the harassment women face when using public transportation.

Other safety concerns are a harsh reality for professional women in emerging markets. In Russia crime is escalating: In one month in 2009 Moscow's murder rate rose by 16% and its fatal assaults by 44%. According to a recent U.S. State Department report, "Assaults and bur-glaries continue to be a part of normal everyday life" in São Paolo and Rio de Janeiro. Rape cases in India rose by more than 30% from 2003 to 2007, and kidnapping or abduction cases rose by more than 50%. These dangers strongly influence women's preferences about what type of career to pursue.

How to Attract and Keep Talented Women

The opportunity has never been greater for multina-tionals to attract and retain top talent in emerging economies. For some it's an imperative. Melinda Wolfe, Bloomberg's head of professional development, says, "Bloomberg is now in 146 countries and growing at a rapid pace. We have an urgent need to draw upon a deep pool of local talent—both men and women—to deliver excellence." Forward-thinking companies can do several things to maximize the opportunity.

Find Talent Early

With so many women earning advanced degrees through-out the developing world, the best place to start looking for talent is the universities. Smart companies adopt a creative and targeted approach, differentiating their brand as employers of choice for talented women. For example, the Google India Women in Engineering Award was launched in 2008 to celebrate women pur-suing engineering and computer sciences careers in college or graduate school. Sixteen women in 2008 and nine in 2009 won the $2,000 award; Google senior

---

The top-talent pool

Percentage of college graduates in 2007 who were women:

UAE 65%

Brazil 60%

United States 58%

China 47%

---

managers and engineers serve as judges. Anjali Sardana, a doctoral candidate at the Indian Institute of Technology (Roorkee), a 2009 winner from among 250 applicants, says that the award has inspired her to keep pursuing her dreams: "Not only did the award encourage me to stay in my field, it has made me confident and given me the spark to mentor other, younger women engineers."

Help Them Build Networks

Ensuring that top talent in emerging markets feels valued is of fundamental importance in multinational organizations, particularly those headquartered in the U.S. or Western Europe. Networking and relationship building, essential to strengthening engagement and commitment, help women develop the ties, visibility, and organizational know-how essential to professional success. Siemens launched a program this year to establish a network for its young, high-potential managers in emerging markets. The company invites them to develop business-centered projects that will contribute to its success; the first plans were presented to Siemens leadership in the spring of 2010.

Women's hours at work

In the countries we studied, educated women working full time at multinational companies say they put in significantly more than 40 hours a week, on average.

73 hours in Russia

71 hours in China

58 hours in India

53 hours in the UAE

49 hours in Brazil

Smart companies are using networks to help women fight isolation and gain visibility as well as achieve their business goals. For instance, General Electric is piloting a version of its myConnections talent-spotting and mentoring program in the UAE. Its goal is to help women connect with one another across levels and functions in the company, recognizing how critical relationships are to career success. The program has been opened up to all of GE's female employees in the UAE. Participants are sorted into "pods" of 10 to 12 members each and assigned a coach, typically a rising female star on the verge of becoming a leader; they determine their own agendas. Four pods have been launched. At one kickoff meeting a woman said that she worked in finance but was based across town from most of her colleagues and felt she was missing out. "I can help you," said another participant, the executive assistant to the region's chief financial officer. As a result, the frustrated finance employee met a senior female finance leader and started building closer ties with her department.

Similarly, Women at Intel Network (WIN) in China, an extension of a global program initiated 13 years ago, endeavors to strike a balance between global goals—in areas ranging from membership to professional development—and local priorities and cultural contexts. In 2007 Intel China became the first to initiate a chapter outside the U.S.; it now has groups in Chengdu, Shanghai, Beijing, and Dalian. "It's not easy for women to have a role in this industry," says Helen Tian, the operations manager of Intel China Research Center and a cohead of the Beijing chapter of WIN. "WIN can bring our women a lot of inspiration to share ideas and help each other on career development."

At monthly meetings the local chapters host visiting senior American women who offer key advice to their Chinese counterparts. For instance, a session on leadership skills and career development in challenging times encouraged women to take on stretch assignments or cross-train with coworkers. In the spring of 2008 Tian helped organize the first Chinese WIN Leadership Development Conference, bringing 300 Intel women together in Shanghai to attend sessions on work/life balance, stress, and technical skills.

Give Them International Exposure

Women are more likely to break through the glass ceiling in multinational companies that make sure they are posted overseas for short periods. However, in emerging markets these assignments work best when companies can provide flexibility and support to lighten the burden on spouses and families. For instance, the

German pharmaceutical giant Boehringer Ingelheim has a short-term assignment program that enables less-mobile employees to gain international exposure. Its assignments—offered around the globe, with a current focus on the Americas—last three to six months and provide development opportunities for high-potential directors and managers. Boehringer Ingelheim supplies housing and transportation in the host country, along with support for family members, including child care, elder care, paid monthly visits for spouses, or opportunities for family members to come along for the entire stay. When a woman from Venezuela took an assignment to Ecuador, Boehringer Ingelheim sent her mother along, too. One woman's stay-at-home husband went with her on assignment to Latin America.

Build Communities Outside the Company

Maximizing opportunities within the company produces great results for professional women, but it's also important to help them build ties to their clients, customers, and communities in emerging markets. These external networks serve two purposes: One is to establish a broader support system for women who are navigating pushes and pulls—particularly important when they have few role models at the top. The other is to strengthen the relationships that help them achieve business results.

The global pharmaceutical giant Pfizer has made it a business priority to engage and retain high-potential female talent in India—one of its top growth markets. The company recently piloted Creating a High Performance

---

How to attract and keep talented women

1. Find talent early. The best place to start looking is in the universities.

2. Help your women recruits build networks to fight isolation and gain visibility while achieving their business goals.

3. Give them international exposure, but provide plenty of support for families in the host countries.

4. Build ties outside the company—to clients, customers, and communities.

Community, under the guidance of its Global Women's Council. The program has three main goals: to ensure that top female talent feels valued and supported; to strengthen connections among Pfizer's high-performing women and their women customers; and to test an approach potentially useful in other markets.

As a starting point, Pfizer India identified its top 10 women in sales and marketing and its 10 most important women customers (including physicians in private practice, medical professionals in high profile hospitals, medical technologists, and so forth). The women participated in a focus group to discuss their career goals and the professional challenges and opportunities they faced. What emerged was a narrative of blazing ambition often blocked by cultural barriers. The women compared notes on the usual issues of work/life balance, but also on how their career aspirations ran contrary to societal expectations. The pilot has established a powerful forum in which Pfizer's rising stars can network with their customers—one where they can celebrate successes and compare difficulties, thus deepening relationships and combating the isolation so frequently experienced by women rising through the ranks. Pfizer India plans to hold a workshop this spring to provide essential career navigation and leadership development skills.

It will be years before the glass ceiling is broken in emerging markets, but some multinational companies are helping to speed up the process by ensuring that they attract and retain the most talented women available. This not only improves the prospects of these companies in developing countries but also has a significant effect on the women they employ. The remarkable reality is that these women are at the forefront of change, shaping the very world in which they live.

SYLVIA ANN HEWLETT is the president and **RIPA RASHID** is a senior vice president of the Center for Work-Life Policy in New York.

Originally published in May 2010. Reprint R1005H

Making Better Investments at the Base of the Pyramid

by Ted London

RAMA WAS A SEAMSTRESS BY TRADE, not an optician. Before she connected with VisionSpring, a venture providing vision care to the poor, she sold hand-sewn clothes and blankets from her home and used her earnings to help support her husband (a farm worker who was often between jobs) and their two children. She took home about $44 a month—not nearly enough to make ends meet. Despite Rama's outgoing personality and strong work ethic, she was unable to drum up increased demand for her handiwork. Then, several years ago, she was trained to be one of VisionSpring's "vision entrepreneurs." Now she is selling eyeglasses and offering vision screenings in her rural Indian community, consistently earning around $100 a month.

Rama's economic turnaround is featured on the website of VisionSpring, which, like a growing number of ventures doing business with the base of the economic pyramid (BoP), shares success stories to demonstrate its results to funders and other stakeholders. These ventures often use anecdotes to highlight how they're helping families build houses in Latin America, providing health-related products to children in Africa, or linking farmers in rural Asia to new markets.

Feel-good stories aside, however, it's been nearly impossible to gauge the efficacy of these ventures. Businesses, nonprofits, and other organizations that deliver products to and purchase goods from the base of the pyramid usually don't have robust-enough systems to accurately assess how well they're reaching the people they set out to serve—or they simply look at the wrong measures. They judge their success at alleviating poverty on the basis of tasks completed and milestones achieved—amount of money invested, quantity of products distributed, number of interventions initiated, and so on—rather than on how well their activities translate into changes on the ground.

While such metrics are potentially useful indicators, they fail to capture the complete picture of a venture's impact. Managers of BoP ventures need to take a more holistic, learning-oriented approach to assessing performance—one that factors in dimensions beyond economic well-being. Consider Rama's situation: Her experience with VisionSpring not only increased her income but also prompted changes within her family. Her husband, who was at first reluctant to support his

Idea in Brief

Though they have feel-good stories and data on milestones, most ventures that serve the world's poor don't have a systematic way to gauge how well they're achieving their goals. To address that need, London, the director of the University of Michigan's Base of the Pyramid Initiative, has devised a new tool. London's Base of the Pyramid Impact Assessment Framework explores how ventures influence the well-being of local buyers, sellers, and communities. It guides managers through a detailed look at an organization's effects on those constituencies in three areas: economics, capabilities, and relationships. The framework examines negative as well as positive effects—for instance, whether activities that increase the income of the poor also prompt them to mistreat arable land. It helps managers focus success measures on the most likely high-magnitude outcomes. VisionSpring, which trains rural women to provide affordable eye care in India, knew it had improved the economic fortunes of its microentrepreneurs. After applying the framework, however, the venture had an appreciation of its impact on some of its buyers: artisans whose eyesight had deteriorated with age. The nonprofit's glasses boosted the artisans' productivity, income, and dignity. VisionSpring also uncovered negative effects— strife and jealousy in families that weren't used to women's working outside the home. The organization helped ease those tensions by encouraging the women's spouses to become involved in product distribution, thus improving their relationships and reducing the risk that sellers might quit. The more holistic, fact-based view provided by London's framework has helped VisionSpring make better decisions about how to enhance positive effects, mitigate negative ones, and demonstrate clear value to potential funders and partners.

wife's work outside the home, decided to join the program once he saw how successful and self-confident Rama had become. Both say their marriage has improved as a result of their working together as a sales team.

After several years of field research, I've developed a framework to help BoP ventures assess the impact their initiatives are having locally, in the short term and over time. It measures how a venture affects the well-being of its critical constituencies in three important dimensions: their economic situation, their capabilities, and their relationships. Whereas traditional monitoring-and-evaluation metrics generally serve to track preestablished milestones and justify past results, this framework can be used as a forward-looking tool. It helps managers identify and enhance the positive effects of a venture's products and services, understand and mitigate the negative effects, and more clearly articulate current performance and prospects for improvement. With this information in hand, they can create more successful, sustainable business models serving the base of the pyramid. Perhaps most important, the framework can amplify for a venture's management team the voices of those living in poverty.

You Are What You Measure

In some ways, the anecdotes about thriving entrepreneurs and other positive outcomes that many ventures tell are akin to the tall tales told by corporations that manipulated their economic returns to present better financial results. That is, by reporting mostly upbeat results, the venture managers fail to present the full range of promises and perils that their activities generate. On the upside, for example, a venture might help local entrepreneurs not only add to their income but also develop new skills and relationships. On the downside, it might promote ineffective or socially inappropriate products, or prompt people to overuse or mistreat community assets, such as arable land or fishing waters. The bottom line: The supporting development agencies, potential funders, and other critical stakeholders of BoP ventures—and even their own managers—usually aren't getting the whole story.

The Base of the Pyramid Impact Assessment Framework keeps the whole story in mind. Over the past three years, I've implemented and refined this framework with partners in corporate, nonprofit, and development sectors in Africa, Asia, and Latin America. It provides a comprehensive process for collecting and analyzing information about the "who" as well as the "how." (See the exhibit "Getting the complete picture.")

Who Is Being Affected?

Any BoP venture potentially affects three groups of local stakeholders: sellers, buyers, and the communities in which it operates. Some ventures use local distributors (sellers) to offer products or services to local consumers (buyers). An example is the Mexican company CEMEX's Patrimonio Hoy initiative, which provides home-building materials to low-income families in Latin America. Other ventures, such as ITC's e-Choupal agricultural initiative in India, rely on local agents (buyers) to act as intermediaries between BoP producers (sellers) and the venture.

Getting the complete picture

The Base of the Pyramid Impact Assessment Framework offers managers of ventures serving the poor a systematic process for measuring—and enhancing—the effects their activities are having on the ground. It involves examining the positive and negative impact those activities have on the well-being of three constituencies: sellers (local distributors or producers), buyers (local consumers or agents), and communities. As a starting point, managers can consider the potential changes listed below, though each organization may have its own unique effects.

Sellers and buyers	Community
Potential changes in economics	
Income and income stability	Incomes of existing businesses as a result of competition
Debt levels; access to credit	Number/type of new businesses serving the community
Productivity (buyers)	
Product pricing, availability, and choice (buyers)	Jobs and economic opportunities
Prices received for products and services (sellers)	Infrastructure
Opportunity costs of not pursuing other livelihoods	
Vulnerability to economic or household shocks	
Potential changes in capabilities	
Skills and knowledge through training and education	Access to free information and educational opportunities
Health and morbidity as a result of involvement with venture or use of product or service	Perceptions about and awareness of opportunities (such as health care and education)
Self-esteem, self-efficacy, and contentment	Sense of dignity and respect
Aspirations and goals	Collective aspirations and goals
Potential changes in relationships	
Access to individuals and networks	Relationship with government and other institutions
Dependence on intermediaries and partner organizations	Gender equity, or views about castes, races, or religions
Reputation, levels of trust, and respect	Social cohesion

Household roles and relationships	Values regarding traditional customs, consumption, and consumerism
Community roles and relationships	
Social status	Relationship with natural environment (ecosystems, land and water quality)

How Are They Being Affected?

It obviously makes sense to focus on an individual or a community's economic well-being (gains or losses in income, assets and liabilities, and so on) when evaluating the effects of a venture. Consumers may get cheaper prices and greater access to needed products and services; producers may enjoy expanded markets and higher productivity; and communities may see a rise in the number of jobs available and companies interested in serving their needs. On the flip side, however, an entrepreneur who decides to invest his own hard-earned capital in a new business may open up himself and his family to unanticipated shocks, such as those generated by health- or crop-related crises. Even when local entrepreneurs do succeed, their actions can still negatively affect the community's economic well-being—for instance, when indigenous businesses suffer because of increased competition.

Ventures focused on the base of the pyramid also affect local capabilities—the skills, health, and confidence individuals and communities need to help themselves and influence the world around them. These capabilities include access to intellectual resources, such as training and education; physical resources, such as clean water and quality medical care; and psychological resources, such as opportunities to influence self-esteem, contentment, and aspirations.

BoP-focused initiatives also shape the relationships of their stakeholders. Indeed, social exclusion and geographic isolation are often components of poverty. BoP ventures can help individuals and communities develop new partnerships and access new networks. They can give individuals and communities a greater voice, which can increase responsiveness and service from the public sector. But they can also encourage greater use of natural resources, damaging the relationship the community has with its local ecosystems.

Additionally, these ventures can prompt people to reconsider their views about gender, ethnicity, and culture. If local women play an important role in the venture, for instance, their status in the family or community may rise. Conversely, ventures serving the base of the pyramid can sometimes significantly disrupt traditional family norms and community perceptions about social structure—and, particularly in the case of gender issues, breed not only discontent but even verbal and physical abuse.

Taking It All In

Implementing the impact assessment tool is a two-stage process. Established ventures, as well as those still in the design phase, can initially use it to conduct a strategic analysis of how their activities can (or will) directly alleviate poverty. Then the venture can use that analysis to develop a set of performance indicators to track the results of initiatives over time, thereby establishing a solid process for continually evaluating what kinds of business models and activities work best and under which conditions.

The Strategic Analysis: Understanding the Impact

Conducting a strategic analysis does not involve an inordinate amount of data crunching. It does require, however, that the venture's assessment team rigorously and collaboratively fill in the cells of the framework. This team, comprising central members of the venture plus any important partners, must list all the expected effects of the venture—both positive and negative—on local stakeholders. How will buyers' personal capabilities be affected—will they be healthier and more self-confident? Will sellers' incomes become more stable? How will critical relationships in the community change as a result of the venture's activities? To avoid double counting, teams should log only direct effects in the framework—noting an increase in, say, buyers' incomes but not how the additional income will or could be spent to improve other aspects of well-being.

The team's ability to fill in all the cells is, of course, contingent upon its ability to listen to and respect the opinions of a variety of stakeholders—field staff, development professionals, academics, and local community members. Those stakeholders should include successful and unsuccessful sellers, happy and disgruntled buyers, aggressive participants in the program and quiet nonparticipants, and pleased and dissatisfied representatives of the community. The team should use a variety of methods to collect data—such as semistructured surveys, focus groups, in-depth discussions, and group forums.

Once the assessment team has a detailed understanding of all the venture's effects, it needs to evaluate each one along two dimensions: its expected magnitude, and the relative likelihood that it will occur. High-magnitude and high-likelihood outcomes should clearly be considered the most important factors in measuring the venture's performance, while low-magnitude and low-likelihood outcomes deserve the least amount of management's attention. The other two categories are less clear-cut, but in general it probably makes sense for venture managers to pay close attention to potentially high-magnitude outcomes even when the likelihood that they will happen is relatively small. Of course, the decision about which critical effects to pay attention to first will depend on the context—which is why it's imperative to consult with the people who face poverty on a daily basis and use their feedback to help set your priorities.

The India team of New York–based VisionSpring used the framework to get a better view of its impact. As alluded to earlier, the venture's microfranchising model helps address the widespread problem of presbyopia, a medical condition most people face as they age, which results in blurry up-close vision. The company recruits "vision entrepreneurs" and gives each a kit—dubbed a "business in a bag"—that contains an initial inventory of 40 pairs of reading glasses of different magnifications and styles, eye-screening materials, marketing resources, and accounting and sales forms. VisionSpring also offers the entrepreneurs several days of training in how to conduct vision screenings, determine the proper power of the glasses needed, make referrals to hospitals if additional eye care is necessary, and manage their inventory. Each entrepreneur is then assigned a cluster of local communities within which to market glasses.

The financial information collected from the entrepreneurs—how many pairs of glasses they sold, the earnings they reported, and so on—showed Vision-Spring's management team that the venture was taking hold in the community. But to expand operations and attract the capital necessary to solve a problem that affects hundreds of millions of individuals globally, VisionSpring's senior leaders knew they would need to develop a more rigorous approach to assessing performance as well as a more robust feedback loop that would help them make better-informed decisions.

So, to get beyond anecdotal evidence, they filled in the cells of the framework. (See the exhibit "One microfranchisor takes inventory.") The group's strategic analysis provided a much clearer articulation of the value VisionSpring created, in particular for buyers. In one district of Andhra Pradesh, for instance, locally produced weavings and other handicrafts were in high demand. Many of the artisans, though, were aging and could no longer see well enough to do the intricate work required. As a result, their incomes declined. Previously, this had been the accepted nature of this occupation; the older you were, the less productive you became. By

One microfranchisor takes inventory

VisionSpring, a venture that employs a microfranchising model to provide eyeglasses and vision screening to the base of the pyramid, used the framework to get a fuller and more accurate picture of the effects it was having locally in India. Here's its assessment of its impact on the well-being of its sellers, buyers, and communities. (Effects are categorized as major or minor on the basis of their expected magnitude and likelihood.)

Sellers (vision entrepreneurs)	Buyers (local consumers)	Communities
Potential changes in economics		
Major effects: Increased income Income instability (lack of guaranteed income) Opportunity costs of not pursuing alternative livelihoods Minor effects: Increased synergy with existing businesses Drop in assets (due to investment in business)	Major effects: Consumer surplus (lower prices and greater convenience) Increased productivity Increased income Minor effects: Savings used or debt incurred (the cost of the glasses)	Minor effects: Increased interest from other businesses in serving the community Drop in existing businesses' income because of increased competition Fewer apprentices enter certain trades because established artisans regain productivity
Potential changes in capabilities		
Major effects: Increased communication skills Better management skills If successful, increased self-efficacy and contentment If unsuccessful, decreased self-efficacy and contentment Minor effects: Increased eye-care skills	Major effects: Improved vision health Increased contentment Minor effects: Treatment for other eye problems through referrals Failure to receive proper diagnosis (eye problems not solved)	Minor effects: Heightened awareness of eye care Greater sense of dignity and respect Higher aspirations of women in the community

Potential changes in relationships		
Major effects: Improved role in family Increased access to networks Stress on family relationships **Minor effects:** Improved relationships within community Stress on relationships within community	**Minor effects:** Better relationships with community and family (less dependent on others) Improved professional reputation	**Major effects:** Greater gender equity **Minor effects:** Improved caste relations Conflict over gender equity issues

providing glasses that improved their near vision, however, VisionSpring allowed these aging artisans to return to a higher level of productivity—and regain their sense of dignity and self-respect. So whereas VisionSpring tended to promote to stakeholders the economic and status gains that its female entrepreneurs were making, the strategic analysis reminded the management team of all the ways that buyers and community members were affected by the venture.

The analysis also helped uncover VisionSpring's potentially negative effects on individuals and the community. For instance, using the framework, the management team was able to recognize the potential for strife and jealousy in families and communities that weren't used to seeing women in nontraditional roles—such as that of an entrepreneur selling wares outside the home and village. Taking those local dynamics into account, VisionSpring offered training to the women's spouses and encouraged them to become more involved in distributing the product—as Rama's husband did. This helped promote the sellers' well-being with regard to relationships and reduced the risk that VisionSpring would lose some of its most successful distributors.

The Performance Analysis: Tracking the Impact

Once the assessment team has completed its strategic analysis, it should have enough information to generate a set of short- and long-term performance metrics to track the activities that are creating the most significant local changes (positive or negative). The findings can also help managers as they work to continually refine the business model to enhance their venture's success.

The process isn't as complicated or expensive as one might think. It involves identifying and collecting baseline as well as post-intervention data on the local buyers, sellers, and communities most affected by the venture's activities, and, whenever possible, on a comparable unaffected group to better account for what would have happened had the venture never launched. The assessment team will have to design data collection approaches that will yield the most useful information, focusing on the "biggest magnitude" and "most likely to occur" indicators revealed by the analysis.

VisionSpring's management team followed up its strategic analysis by working with me and my colleagues at the University of Michigan to develop performance measures. In consultation with a variety of local stakeholders, we created a set of indicators, survey instruments, and a data collection process to track the most relevant effects the venture was having on the three central constituencies. We based some of our survey questions on ones that were previously developed by the World Health Organization and other organizations; we also tailored some to the local situation. We came up with the following.

Sellers. The team members agreed that changes in the sellers' economic situations, capabilities, and relationships could be effectively captured by measuring their incomes (a positive effect), income instability (a negative effect), and opportunity costs of not pursuing other livelihoods (a negative effect); their skills development, self-efficacy, and contentment with life; their perceptions of respect and conflict within the family; and their interactions with individuals and organizations outside their local communities.

Buyers. To measure economic well-being, the team decided it would more closely monitor consumers' incomes, their savings due to product affordability and convenience, and the effect that eyeglasses and vision care had on work productivity. To measure changes in capabilities, the team focused on the role VisionSpring's products and services played in improving buyers' contentment with life and eye health.

Community. The team recognized the importance of changing communities' attitudes toward women who worked as entrepreneurs and took on nontraditional roles outside the home and village.

These measurements helped VisionSpring's management team establish not a selected, anecdotal snapshot of the venture's activities but a holistic and fact-based view—one that clearly showed whom it was helping and how. The framework's findings made it easier for VisionSpring to demonstrate to potential partners the value of investing in the organization.

Missed Opportunities

While VisionSpring used the assessment tool to get the whole story, other ventures—even organizations that have substantial experience working with the base of the pyramid—still rely on less-systematic means to assess the efficacy of their activities, missing out on opportunities to have even greater impact. Consider the initiative piloted in India by Pioneer Hi-Bred International (a subsidiary of DuPont), the Peoples Action for Creative Education (PEACE), and CARE. The program, based near the city of Hyderabad, allowed Pioneer to distribute its seeds to village farmers through PEACE, a local nonprofit. CARE, an international relief and development nonprofit, facilitated the relationship between the two other organizations.

Agriculture is the primary source of local income in rural India and the predominant work activity, but productivity is low in some communities—in part because farmers have limited access to high-quality supplies and equipment. Take seeds: Farmers in India had traditionally set aside the seeds harvested from one year's crop to plant the next year. These days farmers increasingly buy their seeds from local traders who specialize in selling a wide range of farming supplies—albeit sometimes counterfeit or low-quality goods. The traders obviously can be a risky channel for the farmer;

bad seeds translate into a bad harvest. Because the farmers are rarely able to save much income from previous years, they must take out expensive loans at the beginning of each planting season to pay for supplies.

The partnership set out to provide farmers with high-quality, high-yield maize seeds resistant to waterlogging. The seeds cost more per acre to plant initially, but expected productivity gains justified the added expense. Recognizing that the outlay for seeds might be relatively expensive, PEACE didn't ask the farmers to pay for them until after the harvest.

The partners knew it would take time for the seeds to be accepted and had figured the pilot would be more of a learning experience than a profit-making one. Yet after the first harvest, the initiative had gained only limited traction with local farmers. If the partners had undertaken a strategic analysis of the venture's effects on poverty alleviation, specifically looking at economics, capabilities, and relationships, they might have gained the following insights about its initial business model. (See the exhibit "A farming initiative's business model shows holes.")

Economics
Through the partnership, the farmers got a higher-quality product under payback terms that were sensitive to the seasonality of their business—but they still had to deal with indebtedness. In fact, doing business with the venture put them at greater economic risk, given the larger initial investment required. If the monsoons were late or flooding occurred, all or a portion of

A farming initiative's business model shows holes

Working with local development partners CARE and PEACE, Pioneer Hi-Bred International set up a venture designed to serve the needs of poor farmers, focusing in particular on providing them with high-quality seeds. However, its business model didn't account for some important constraints the farmers, or buyers, faced—as shown by the major negative effects on well-being in the framework below. (Since PEACE is the distributor/agent, the effects on sellers are not included in the framework.)

Buyers (farmers)	Community
Potential changes in economics	
Major effects:	Major effects:
Increased productivity (from high-quality, high-yield seeds)	Drop in income of local traders
More income stability (protection from water damage)	Minor effects:
Uncertain crop prices (especially if increases in supply are not met with increases in demand)	Increased interest by other businesses in serving the community
Increased debt and greater vulnerability to economic or household shocks	
Minor effects:	
Improved cash flow (loan repayment tied to harvest season)	
Improved cost of capital (interest rates)	
Potential changes in capabilities	
Major effects:	Minor effects:
More dignity and respect (from having increased choice)	Openness to innovations and new farming techniques
Improved aspirations (if harvest goes well)	Improved aspirations of all community members
Uncertainty and stress (from relying on a new product)	
Drop in aspirations (if harvest is poor)	
Minor effects:	
Time and energy savings (from using high-quality seeds)	

Potential changes in relationships	
Major effects:	**Major effects:**
Increased status in family (women receive the seeds)	Greater gender equity
Retaliation by local traders	**Minor effects:**
Conflicts within families	Less use of indigenous seeds harvested from prior year's crop
Minor effects:	Effect of planting hybrid seeds on local ecosystems
Increased networking with others outside the community	Conflict over gender equity issues
Increased dependence on outside products and suppliers	

their crops would be lost—sure disaster for rural farming families, who often don't have a financial safety net. The partnership's business model also didn't address the challenges that farmers face in selling what they harvest. They have to accept whatever price the market sets for their produce, after all, and are vulnerable to changes in demand.

Capabilities and Relationships
Pioneer's seeds at first were an unknown in the eyes of the local community; the farmers weren't sure how best to use them to maximize their yields. And the farmers still faced a relationship with monopolistic local intermediaries. If the farmers were too selective about the products they were buying—getting their seeds from PEACE instead of the local traders, for instance—they could find themselves cut off, unable to procure the rest of their farming supplies from traders bearing grudges.

The framework makes it clear: Until these concerns are addressed by the venture's business design— something Pioneer and its partners, to their credit, have continued to work on—adoption of the seeds will most likely remain modest, thus limiting the venture's prospects for creating value for itself and for farmers at the base of the pyramid.

———————

Anecdotes can capture our imagination. Data from monitoring and evaluation efforts can be used to track specific milestones and financial outcomes against plan. But the lack of a systematic and holistic approach to assessing and enhancing the performance of BoP ventures does a great disservice not only to those living in poverty but to the ventures themselves. After all, the better a business understands its target market, the better it should perform.

The primary purpose of the BoP Impact Assessment Framework is to give managers a standardized approach for understanding the whole story. For managers, development groups, and funders, it can also generate some important insights into the types of organizational designs that are most likely to succeed with the base of the pyramid. Indeed, the framework could be a powerful new lens for organizations that have tough decisions to make about how and where to invest. They can use the framework to evaluate a management team's understanding of a venture's on-the-ground impact, for instance, or to make the case for supporting carefully targeted ventures that are in line with their own philosophies about alleviating poverty— those that, say, are best at empowering women or connecting previously isolated communities to the outside world.

For far too long now, the lack of a dynamic and inclusive process for hearing and responding to the voices of the base of the pyramid, coupled with a lack of humility from many organizations and ventures at the top, has limited the effectiveness of initiatives serving the poor. It is time for a change.

TED LONDON is the director of the University of Michigan's Base of the Pyramid Initiative and serves on the faculty of the university's Stephen M. Ross School of Business.

Originally published in May 2009. Reprint R0905J

Strategies That Fit Emerging Markets

by Tarun Khanna, Krishna G. Palepu, and Jayant Sinha

CEOS AND TOP MANAGEMENT TEAMS of large corporations, particularly in North America, Europe, and Japan, acknowledge that globalization is the most critical challenge they face today. They are also keenly aware that it has become tougher during the past decade to identify internationalization strategies and to choose which countries to do business with. Still, most companies have stuck to the strategies they've traditionally deployed, which emphasize standardized approaches to new markets while sometimes experimenting with a few local twists. As a result, many multinational corporations are struggling to develop successful strategies in emerging markets.

Part of the problem, we believe, is that the absence of specialized intermediaries, regulatory systems, and contract-enforcing mechanisms in emerging markets—"institutional voids," we christened them in a 1997 HBR article—hampers the implementation of globalization strategies. Companies in developed countries usually take for granted the critical role that "soft" infrastructure plays in the execution of their business models in their home markets. But that infrastructure is often underdeveloped or absent in emerging markets. There's no dearth of examples. Companies can't find skilled market research firms to inform them reliably about customer preferences so they can tailor products to specific needs and increase people's willingness to pay. Few end-to-end logistics providers, which allow manufacturers to reduce costs, are available to transport raw materials and finished products. Before recruiting employees, corporations have to screen large numbers of candidates themselves because there aren't many search firms that can do the job for them.

Because of all those institutional voids, many multinational companies have fared poorly in developing countries. All the anecdotal evidence we have gathered suggests that since the 1990s, American corporations have performed better in their home environments than they have in foreign countries, especially in emerging markets. Not surprisingly, many CEOs are wary of emerging markets and prefer to invest in developed nations instead. By the end of 2002—according to the Bureau of Economic Analysis, an agency of the U.S. Department of Commerce—American corporations and their affiliate companies had $1.6 trillion worth of assets in the United Kingdom and $514 billion in Canada but only $173 billion in Brazil, Russia, India, and China combined. That's just 2.5% of the $6.9 trillion in investments American companies held by the end of that year.

Idea in Brief

What's the fastest-growing market in the world for most products and services? Developing countries. Yet many companies shy away from doing business in these nations. CEOs are all too aware that such countries lack the market institutions needed to do business successfully—such as consumer-data experts, end-to-end logistics providers, and talent search firms.

But avoid investing in developing countries, and you won't remain competitive for long. How to mitigate the risks? As authors Khanna, Palepu, and Sinha recommend, first analyze each country's **institutional context,** including political and social systems; openness to foreign investment; and quality of product, labor, and capital markets.

Then decide: Should you work around your target country's institutional weaknesses? Create new market infrastructures (for example, your own in-country supply chain)? Or stay away because adapting your business model would be impractical or uneconomical?

Dell Computer chose to adapt its business model to enter China. After discovering that Chinese consumers didn't buy over the Internet (a cornerstone of Dell's North American business model), Dell sold its products through Chinese distributors and systems integrators.

Correctly diagnose developing countries' institutional contexts, and you make savvier foreign-investment decisions. You avoid markets you can't profitably serve—while capturing the wealth of opportunities presented by other emerging markets.

In fact, although U.S. corporations' investments in China doubled between 1992 and 2002, that amount was still less than 1% of all their overseas assets.

Many companies shied away from emerging markets when they should have engaged with them more closely. Since the early 1990s, developing countries have been the fastest-growing market in the world for most products

Idea in Practice

Diagnose Institutional Contexts

Criterion	Sample questions	Example: Brazil
Political and social systems	• How is power distributed among the central, state, and city governments? • Do laws protect private property rights? • Is the judiciary independent?	Has a vibrant democracy, though pockets of corruption exist in federal and state governments.
Openness	• What restrictions does the government place on foreign investments? • How cumbersome are procedures for launching new ventures?	Outside companies partner with locals to gain local expertise.
Product markets	• Can you obtain reliable data on consumer preferences? • Is there a deep network of suppliers? • How strong are transportation infrastructures?	Suppliers available in the Mercosur region. Good network of highways, airports, and ports.
Labor markets	• How strong are educational institutions, especially for technical and management training? • Do people do business in English? • Is pay for performance standard practice?	Managers have varying degrees of proficiency in English. Trade unions are strong.
Capital markets	• How effectively do banks collect savings and channel them into investments? • How reliable is corporate performance information?	Bankruptcy processes are inefficient, while financial-reporting systems function well.

Decide Your Strategy

Based on your target's institutional context, decide whether you'll:

- **Adapt your business model:** Ensure that changes to your model preserve your competitive advantage.

  Example: In the U.S., McDonald's outsources supply chain operations. But when it tried to enter Russia, it couldn't find local suppliers. So, with help from its joint venture partner, it identified farmers it could work with and advanced them money so they could invest in seeds and equipment. And it sent Russian managers to Canada for training. By establishing its own supply chain and management systems, it now controls 80% of the Russian fast-food market.

- **Change the institutional context:** A powerful company's products or services can force dramatic improvements in local markets. For example,

  when Big Four audit firms set up branches in Brazil, their presence raised countrywide financial-reporting and auditing standards. That in turn gave multinationals with Brazilian subsidiaries access to global-quality audit services.

- **Stay away:** If adapting your business model is impractical, avoid investing.

  Example: Home Depot's value proposition (low prices, great service, good quality) hinges on many U.S.-specific institutions—including reliable transportation networks to minimize inventory and employee stock ownership to motivate workers to provide top-notch service. It avoids countries with weak logistics systems and poorly developed capital markets, where it would have difficulty using its inventory management system and may not be able to use employee stock ownership.

and services. Companies can lower costs by setting up manufacturing facilities and service centers in those areas, where skilled labor and trained managers are relatively inexpensive. Moreover, several developing-country transnational corporations have entered North America and Europe with low-cost strategies (China's Haier Group in household electrical appliances) and novel business models (India's Infosys in information technology services). Western companies that want to develop counterstrategies must push deeper into emerging markets, which foster a different genre of innovations than mature markets do.

If Western companies don't develop strategies for engaging across their value chains with developing countries, they are unlikely to remain competitive for long. However, despite crumbling tariff barriers, the spread of the Internet and cable television, and the rapidly improving physical infrastructure in these countries, CEOs can't assume they can do business in emerging markets the same way they do in developed nations. That's because the quality of the market infrastructure varies widely from country to country. In general, advanced economies have large pools of seasoned market intermediaries and effective contract-enforcing mechanisms, whereas less-developed economies have unskilled intermediaries and less-effective legal systems. Because the services provided by intermediaries either aren't available in emerging markets or aren't very sophisticated, corporations can't smoothly transfer the strategies they employ in their home countries to those emerging markets.

During the past ten years, we've researched and consulted with multinational corporations all over the world. One of us led a comparative research project on China and India at Harvard Business School, and we have all been involved in McKinsey & Company's Global Champions research project. We have learned that successful companies work around institutional voids. They develop strategies for doing business in emerging markets that are different from those they use at home and often find novel ways of implementing them, too. They also customize their approaches to fit each nation's institutional context. As we will show, firms that take the trouble to understand the institutional differences between countries are likely to choose the best markets to enter, select optimal strategies, and make the most out of operating in emerging markets.

Why Composite Indices Are Inadequate

Before we delve deeper into institutional voids, it's important to understand why companies often target the wrong countries or deploy inappropriate globalization strategies. Many corporations enter new lands because of senior managers' personal experiences, family ties, gut feelings, or anecdotal evidence. Others follow key customers or rivals into emerging markets; the herd instinct is strong among multinationals. Biases, too, dog companies' foreign investments. For instance, the reason U.S. companies preferred to do business with China rather than India for decades was probably because of America's romance with China, first profiled in MIT political scientist Harold Isaacs's work in the late 1950s. Isaacs pointed out that partly as a result of the work missionaries and scholars did in China in the 1800s, Americans became more familiar with China than with India.

Companies that choose new markets systematically often use tools like country portfolio analysis and political risk assessment, which chiefly focus on the potential profits from doing business in developing countries but leave out essential information about the soft infrastructures there. In December 2004, when the McKinsey Global Survey of Business Executives polled 9,750 senior managers on their priorities and concerns, 61% said that market size and growth drove their firms' decisions to enter new countries. While 17% felt that political and economic stability was the most important factor in making those decisions, only 13% said that structural conditions (in other words, institutional contexts) mattered most.

Just how do companies estimate a nation's potential? Executives usually analyze its GDP and per capita income growth rates, its population composition and growth rates, and its exchange rates and purchasing power parity indices (past, present, and projected). To complete the picture, managers consider the nation's standing on the World Economic Forum's Global Competitiveness Index, the World Bank's governance indicators, and Transparency International's corruption ratings; its weight in emerging market funds investments; and, perhaps, forecasts of its next political transition.

Such composite indices are no doubt useful, but companies should use them as the basis for drawing up strategies only when their home bases and target countries have comparable institutional contexts. For example, the United States and the United Kingdom have similar product, capital, and labor markets, with networks of skilled intermediaries and strong regulatory systems. The two nations share an Anglo-Saxon legal system as well. American companies can enter Britain comfortable in the knowledge that they will find competent market research firms, that they can count on English law to enforce agreements they sign with potential partners, and that retailers will be able to distribute products all over the country. Those are dangerous assumptions to make in an emerging market, where skilled intermediaries or contract-enforcing mechanisms are unlikely to be found. However, composite indices don't flash warning signals to would-be entrants about the presence of institutional voids in emerging markets.

In fact, composite index–based analyses of developing countries conceal more than they reveal. (See the exhibit "The trouble with composite indices.") In 2003, Brazil, Russia, India, and China appeared similar on several indices. Yet despite the four countries' comparable standings, the key success factors in each of those markets have turned out to be very different. For instance, in China and Russia, multinational retail chains and local retailers have expanded into the urban and semi-urban areas, whereas in Brazil, only a few global chains have set up shop in key urban centers. And in India, the government prohibited foreign direct investment in the retailing and real estate industries until February 2005, so mom-and-pop retailers dominate. Brazil, Russia,

The trouble with composite indices

Companies often base their globalization strategies on country rankings, but on most lists, it is impossible to tell developing countries apart. According to the six indices below, Brazil, India, and China share similar markets while Russia, though an outlier on many parameters, is comparable to the other nations. Contrary to what these rankings suggest, however, the market infrastructure in each of these countries varies widely, and companies need to deploy very different strategies to succeed.

	Brazil	Russia	India	China
Growth Competitiveness Index ranking* (out of 104 countries; for 2003)	7	70	55	46
Business Competitiveness Index ranking* (out of 103 countries; for 2003)	8	61	30	47
Governance indicators (percentile rankings)** (out of 199 countries; for 2002)				
Voice and accountability	58.1	33.8	60.2	10.1
Political stability	48.1	33.0	22.2	51.4
Government effectiveness	50.0	44.3	54.1	63.4
Regulatory quality	63.4	44.3	43.8	40.2
Rule of law	50.0	25.3	57.2	51.5
Control of corruption	56.7	21.1	49.5	42.3
Corruption Perceptions Index ranking*** (out of 145 countries; for 2004)	59	90	90	71
Composite Country Risk points**** (for January 2005; the larger the number, the less risky the country)	70	78	72	76
Weight in Emerging Markets Index (%)***** (for February 2004; out of 26 emerging markets)	6.96%	5.16%	5.02%	4.76%

Sources: * World Economic Forum, "Global Competitiveness Report," 2004–2005
** World Bank Governance Research Indicator Country Snapshot, 2002
*** Transparency International, Corruption Perceptions Index, 2004
**** The PRS Group, *International Country Risk Guide,* January 2005
***** Barclays Global Investors, iShares "2004 Semi-Annual Report to Shareholders"

India, and China may all be big markets for multinational consumer product makers, but executives have to design unique distribution strategies for each market. That process must start with a thorough understanding of the differences between the countries' market infrastructures. Those differences may make it more attractive for some businesses to enter, say, Brazil than India.

How to Map Institutional Contexts

As we helped companies think through their globalization strategies, we came up with a simple conceptual device—the five contexts framework—that lets executives map the institutional contexts of any country. Economics 101 tells us that companies buy inputs in the product, labor, and capital markets and sell their outputs in the products (raw materials and finished goods) or services market. When choosing strategies, therefore, executives need to figure out how the product, labor, and capital markets work—and don't work—in their target countries. This will help them understand the differences between home markets and those in developing countries. In addition, each country's social and political milieu—as well as the manner in which it has opened up to the outside world—shapes those markets, and companies must consider those factors, too.

The five contexts framework places a superstructure of key markets on a base of sociopolitical choices. Many multinational corporations look at either the macro factors (the degree of openness and the sociopolitical atmosphere) or some of the market factors, but few pay

Spotting Institutional Voids

MANAGERS CAN IDENTIFY the institutional voids in any country by asking a series of questions. The answers—or sometimes, the lack of them—will tell companies where they should adapt their business models to the nation's institutional context.

Political and Social System

1. To whom are the country's politicians accountable? Are there strong political groups that oppose the ruling party? Do elections take place regularly?

2. Are the roles of the legislative, executive, and judiciary clearly defined? What is the distribution of power between the central, state, and city governments?

3. Does the government go beyond regulating business to interfering in it or running companies?

4. Do the laws articulate and protect private property rights?

5. What is the quality of the country's bureaucrats? What are bureaucrats' incentives and career trajectories?

6. Is the judiciary independent? Do the courts adjudicate disputes and enforce contracts in a timely and impartial manner? How effective are the quasi-judicial regulatory institutions that set and enforce rules for business activities?

7. Do religious, linguistic, regional, and ethnic groups coexist peacefully, or are there tensions between them?

8. How vibrant and independent is the media? Are newspapers and magazines neutral, or do they represent sectarian interests?

9. Are nongovernmental organizations, civil rights groups, and environmental groups active in the country?

10. Do people tolerate corruption in business and government?

11. What role do family ties play in business?

12. Can strangers be trusted to honor a contract in the country?

Openness

1. Are the country's government, media, and people receptive to foreign investment? Do citizens trust companies and individuals from some parts of the world more than others?

2. What restrictions does the government place on foreign investment? Are those restrictions in place to facilitate the growth of domestic companies, to protect state monopolies, or because people are suspicious of multinationals?

3. Can a company make greenfield investments and acquire local companies, or can it only break into the market by entering into joint ventures? Will that company be free to choose partners based purely on economic considerations?

4. Does the country allow the presence of foreign intermediaries such as market research and advertising firms, retailers, media companies, banks, insurance companies, venture capital firms, auditing firms, management consulting firms, and educational institutions?

5. How long does it take to start a new venture in the country? How cumbersome are the government's procedures for permitting the launch of a wholly foreign-owned business?

6. Are there restrictions on portfolio investments by overseas companies or on dividend repatriation by multinationals?

7. Does the market drive exchange rates, or does the government control them? If it's the latter, does the government try to maintain a stable exchange rate, or does it try to favor domestic products over imports by propping up the local currency?

8. What would be the impact of tariffs on a company's capital goods and raw materials imports? How would import duties affect that company's ability to manufacture its products locally versus exporting them from home?

(continued)

Spotting Institutional Voids (continued)

9. Can a company set up its business anywhere in the country? If the government restricts the company's location choices, are its motives political, or is it inspired by a logical regional development strategy?

10. Has the country signed free-trade agreements with other nations? If so, do those agreements favor investments by companies from some parts of the world over others?

11. Does the government allow foreign executives to enter and leave the country freely? How difficult is it to get work permits for managers and engineers?

12. Does the country allow its citizens to travel abroad freely? Can ideas flow into the country unrestricted? Are people permitted to debate and accept those ideas?

Product Markets

1. Can companies easily obtain reliable data on customer tastes and purchase behaviors? Are there cultural barriers to market research? Do world-class market research firms operate in the country?

2. Can consumers easily obtain unbiased information on the quality of the goods and services they want to buy? Are there independent consumer organizations and publications that provide such information?

3. Can companies access raw materials and components of good quality? Is there a deep network of suppliers? Are there firms that assess suppliers' quality and reliability? Can companies enforce contracts with suppliers?

4. How strong are the logistics and transportation infrastructures? Have global logistics companies set up local operations?

5. Do large retail chains exist in the country? If so, do they cover the entire country or only the major cities? Do they reach all consumers or only wealthy ones?

6. Are there other types of distribution channels, such as direct-to-consumer channels and discount retail channels, that deliver products to customers?

7. Is it difficult for multinationals to collect receivables from local retailers?

8. Do consumers use credit cards, or does cash dominate transactions? Can consumers get credit to make purchases? Are data on customer creditworthiness available?

9. What recourse do consumers have against false claims by companies or defective products and services?

10. How do companies deliver after-sales service to consumers? Is it possible to set up a nationwide service network? Are third-party service providers reliable?

11. Are consumers willing to try new products and services? Do they trust goods from local companies? How about from foreign companies?

12. What kind of product-related environmental and safety regulations are in place? How do the authorities enforce those regulations?

Labor Markets

1. How strong is the country's education infrastructure, especially for technical and management training? Does it have a good elementary and secondary education system as well?

2. Do people study and do business in English or in another international language, or do they mainly speak a local language?

3. Are data available to help sort out the quality of the country's educational institutions?

4. Can employees move easily from one company to another? Does the local culture support that movement? Do recruitment agencies facilitate executive mobility?

(*continued*)

Spotting Institutional Voids (continued)

5. What are the major postrecruitment-training needs of the people that multinationals hire locally?

6. Is pay for performance a standard practice? How much weight do executives give seniority, as opposed to merit, in making promotion decisions?

7. Would a company be able to enforce employment contracts with senior executives? Could it protect itself against executives who leave the firm and then compete against it? Could it stop employees from stealing trade secrets and intellectual property?

8. Does the local culture accept foreign managers? Do the laws allow a firm to transfer locally hired people to another country? Do managers want to stay or leave the nation?

9. How are the rights of workers protected? How strong are the country's trade unions? Do they defend workers' interests or only advance a political agenda?

10. Can companies use stock options and stock-based compensation schemes to motivate employees?

11. Do the laws and regulations limit a firm's ability to restructure, downsize, or shut down?

12. If a company were to adopt its local rivals' or suppliers' business practices, such as the use of child labor, would that tarnish its image overseas?

Capital Markets

1. How effective are the country's banks, insurance companies, and mutual funds at collecting savings and channeling them into investments?

2. Are financial institutions managed well? Is their decision making transparent? Do noneconomic considerations, such as family ties, influence their investment decisions?

3. Can companies raise large amounts of equity capital in the stock market? Is there a market for corporate debt?

4. Does a venture capital industry exist? If so, does it allow individuals with good ideas to raise funds?

5. How reliable are sources of information on company performance? Do the accounting standards and disclosure regulations permit investors and creditors to monitor company management?

6. Do independent financial analysts, rating agencies, and the media offer unbiased information on companies?

7. How effective are corporate governance norms and standards at protecting shareholder interests?

8. Are corporate boards independent and empowered, and do they have independent directors?

9. Are regulators effective at monitoring the banking industry and stock markets?

10. How well do the courts deal with fraud?

11. Do the laws permit companies to engage in hostile takeovers? Can shareholders organize themselves to remove entrenched managers through proxy fights?

12. Is there an orderly bankruptcy process that balances the interests of owners, creditors, and other stakeholders?

attention to both. We have developed sets of questions that companies can ask to create a map of each country's context and to gauge the extent to which businesses must adapt their strategies to each one. (See the sidebar "Spotting Institutional Voids.") Before we apply the framework to some developing countries, let's briefly touch on the five contexts.

Political and Social Systems

As we've discussed, every country's political system affects its product, labor, and capital markets. In socialist societies like China, for instance, workers cannot form independent trade unions in the labor market, which affects wage levels. A country's social environment is also important. In South Africa, for example, the government's support for the transfer of assets to the historically disenfranchised native African community—a laudable social objective—has affected the development of the capital market. Such transfers usually price assets in an arbitrary fashion, which makes it hard for multinationals to figure out the value of South African companies and affects their assessments of potential partners.

The thorny relationships between ethnic, regional, and linguistic groups in emerging markets also affects foreign investors. In Malaysia, for instance, foreign companies should enter into joint ventures only after checking if their potential partners belong to the majority Malay community or the economically dominant Chinese community, so as not to conflict with the government's long-standing policy of transferring some assets from Chinese to Malays. This policy arose because of a perception that the race riots of 1969 were caused by the tension between the Chinese haves and the Malay have-nots. Although the rhetoric has changed somewhat in the past few years, the pro-Malay policy remains in place.

Executives would do well to identify a country's power centers, such as its bureaucracy, media, and civil society, and figure out if there are checks and balances in place. Managers must also determine how decentralized the political system is, if the government is subject to oversight, and whether bureaucrats and politicians are independent from one another. Companies should gauge the level of actual trust among the populace as opposed to enforced trust. For instance, if people believe companies won't vanish with their savings, firms may be able to raise money locally sooner rather than later.

Openness

CEOs often talk about the need for economies to be open because they believe it's best to enter countries that welcome direct investment by multinational corporations— although companies can get into countries that don't allow foreign investment by entering into joint ventures or by licensing local partners. Still, they must remember that the concept of "open" can be deceptive. For example, executives believe that China is an open economy because the government welcomes foreign investment but that India is a relatively closed economy because of the lukewarm reception the Indian government gives multinationals. However, India has been open to ideas from the West, and people have always been able to travel freely in and out of the country, whereas for decades, the Chinese government didn't allow its citizens to travel abroad freely, and it still doesn't allow many ideas to cross its borders. Consequently, while it may be true that multinational companies can invest in

China more easily than they can in India, managers in India are more inclined to be market oriented and globally aware than managers are in China.

The more open a country's economy, the more likely it is that global intermediaries will be allowed to operate there. Multinationals, therefore, will find it easier to function in markets that are more open because they can use the services of both the global and local intermediaries. However, openness can be a double-edged sword: A government that allows local companies to access the global capital market neutralizes one of foreign companies' key advantages.

The two macro contexts we have just described— political and social systems and openness—shape the market contexts. For instance, in Chile, a military coup in the early 1970s led to the establishment of a right-wing government, and that government's liberal economic policies led to a vibrant capital market in the country. But Chile's labor market remained underdeveloped because the government did not allow trade unions to operate freely. Similarly, openness affects the development of markets. If a country's capital markets are open to foreign investors, financial intermediaries will become more sophisticated. That has happened in India, for example, where capital markets are more open than they are in China. Likewise, in the product market, if multinationals can invest in the retail industry, logistics providers will develop rapidly. This has been the case in China, where providers have taken hold more quickly than they have in India, which has only recently allowed multinationals to invest in retailing.

Product Markets

Developing countries have opened up their markets and grown rapidly during the past decade, but companies still struggle to get reliable information about consumers, especially those with low incomes. Developing a consumer finance business is tough, for example, because the data sources and credit histories that firms draw on in the West don't exist in emerging markets. Market research and advertising are in their infancy in developing countries, and it's difficult to find the deep databases on consumption patterns that allow companies to segment consumers in more-developed markets. There are few government bodies or independent publications, like *Consumer Reports* in the United States, that provide expert advice on the features and quality of products. Because of a lack of consumer courts and advocacy groups in developing nations, many people feel they are at the mercy of big companies.

Labor Markets

In spite of emerging markets' large populations, multinationals have trouble recruiting managers and other skilled workers because the quality of talent is hard to ascertain. There are relatively few search firms and recruiting agencies in low-income countries. The high-quality firms that do exist focus on top-level searches, so companies must scramble to identify middle-level managers, engineers, or floor supervisors. Engineering colleges, business schools, and training institutions have proliferated, but apart from an elite few, there's no way for companies to tell which schools produce skilled managers. For instance, several Indian companies have sprung up to train people for jobs in the call center business, but no organization rates the quality of the training it provides.

Capital Markets

The capital and financial markets in developing countries are remarkable for their lack of sophistication. Apart from a few stock exchanges and government-appointed regulators, there aren't many reliable intermediaries like credit-rating agencies, investment analysts, merchant bankers, or venture capital firms. Multinationals can't count on raising debt or equity capital locally to finance their operations. Like investors, creditors don't have access to accurate information on companies. Businesses can't easily assess the creditworthiness of other firms or collect receivables after they have extended credit to customers. Corporate governance is also notoriously poor in emerging markets. Transnational companies, therefore, can't trust their partners to adhere to local laws and joint venture agreements. In fact, since crony capitalism thrives in developing countries, multinationals can't assume that the profit motive alone is what's driving local firms.

Several CEOs have asked us why we emphasize the role of institutional intermediaries and ignore industry factors. They argue that industry structure, such as the degree of competition, should also influence companies' strategies. But when Harvard Business School professor Jan Rivkin and one of the authors of this article ranked industries by profitability, they found that the correlation of industry rankings across pairs of countries was close to zero, which means that the attractiveness of an industry varied widely from country to country. So although factors like scale economies, entry barriers, and the ability to differentiate products matter in every industry, the weight of their importance varies from place to place. An attractive industry in your home market may turn out to be unattractive in another country. Companies should analyze industry structures—always a useful exercise—only after they understand a country's institutional context.

Applying the Framework

When we applied the five contexts framework to emerging markets in four countries—Brazil, Russia, India, and China—the differences between them became apparent. (See the exhibit "Mapping contexts in Brazil, Russia, India, and China.") Multinationals face different kinds of competition in each of those nations. In China, state-owned enterprises control nearly half the economy, members of the Chinese diaspora control many of the foreign corporations that operate there, and the private sector brings up the rear because entrepreneurs find it almost impossible to access capital. India is the mirror image of China. Public sector corporations, though important, occupy nowhere near as prominent a place as they do in China. Unlike China, India is wary of foreign investment, even by members of the Indian diaspora. However, the country has spawned many private sector organizations, some of which are

Mapping contexts in Brazil, Russia, India, and China

The five contexts (below) can help companies spot the institutional voids in any country. An application of the framework to the four fastest-growing markets in the world reveals how different those countries are from developed nations and, more important, from one another.

Political and social system

U.S./EU	Brazil	Russia	India	China
Political structure				
Countries have vibrant democracies with checks and balances. Companies can count on rule of law and fair enforcement of legal contracts.	The democracy is vibrant. Bureaucracy is rampant. There are pockets of corruption in federal and state governments.	A centralized government and some regional fiefdoms coexist. Bureaucracy is stifling. Corruption occurs at all levels of government.	The democracy is vibrant. The government is highly bureaucratic. Corruption is rampant in state and local governments.	The Communist Party maintains a monopoly on political power. Local governments make economic policy decisions. Officials may abuse power for personal gain.
Civil society				
A dynamic media acts as a check on abuses by both companies and governments. Powerful nongovernmental organizations (NGOs) influence corporate policies on social and environmental issues.	Influential local media serves as a watchdog. The influence of local NGOs is marginal.	The media is controlled by the government. NGOs are underdeveloped and disorganized.	A dynamic press and vigilant NGOs act as checks on politicians and companies.	The media is muzzled by the government, and there are few independent NGOs. Companies don't have to worry about criticism, but they can't count on civil society to check abuses of power.

Openness

U.S./EU	Brazil	Russia	India	China
Modes of entry				
Open to all forms of foreign investment except when governments have concerns about potential monopolies or national security issues.	Both greenfield investments and acquisitions are possible entry strategies. Companies team up with local partners to gain local expertise.	Both greenfield investments and acquisitions are possible but difficult. Companies form alliances to gain access to government and local inputs.	Restrictions on greenfield investments and acquisitions in some sectors make joint ventures necessary. Red tape hinders companies in sectors where the government does allow foreign investment.	The government permits greenfield investments as well as acquisitions. Acquired companies are likely to have been state owned and may have hidden liabilities. Alliances let companies align interests with all levels of government.

Product markets

U.S./EU	Brazil	Russia	India	China
Product development and intellectual property rights (IPR)				
Sophisticated product-design capabilities are available. Governments enforce IPR and protect trademarks, so R&D investments yield competitive advantages.	Local design capability exists. IPR disputes with the United States exist in some sectors.	The country has a strong local design capability but exhibits an ambivalent attitude about IPR. Sufficient regulatory authority exists, but enforcement is patchy.	Some local design capability is available. IPR problems with the United States exist in some industries. Regulatory bodies monitor product quality and fraud.	Imitation and piracy abound. Punishment for IPR theft varies across provinces and by level of corruption.

(continued)

Mapping contexts in Brazil, Russia, India, and China (continued)

Product markets (continued)

U.S./EU	Brazil	Russia	India	China
Supplier base and logistics				
Companies use national and international suppliers. Firms outsource and move manufacturing and services offshore instead of integrating vertically. A highly developed.	Suppliers are available in the Mercosur region. A good network of highways, airports, and ports exists.	Companies can rely on local suppliers for simple components. The European region has decent logistics networks, but trans-Ural Russia is not well developed.	Suppliers are available, but their quality and dependability varies greatly. Roads are in poor condition. Ports and airports are underdeveloped.	Several suppliers have strong manufacturing capabilities, but few vendors have advanced technical abilities. The road network is well developed. Port facilities
Brand perceptions and management				
Markets are mature and have strong local and global brands. The profusion of brands clutters consumer choice. Numerous ad agencies are available.	Consumers accept both local and global brands. Global as well as local ad agencies are present.	Consumers prefer global brands in automobiles and high tech. Local brands thrive in the food and beverage businesses. Some local and global ad agencies are available.	Consumers buy both local and global brands. Global ad agencies are present, but they have been less successful than local ad agencies.	Consumers prefer to buy products from American, European, and Japanese companies. Multinational ad agencies dominate the business.

Labor markets

U.S./EU	Brazil	Russia	India	China
Market for managers				
A large and varied pool of well-trained management talent exists.	The large pool of management talent has varying degrees of proficiency in English. Both local and expatriate managers hold senior management jobs.	The large pool of management talent has varying degrees of proficiency in English, and it is supplemented by expatriate managers. Employment agencies are booming.	The country has a highly liquid pool of English-speaking management talent fueled by business and technical schools. Local hires are preferred over expatriates.	There is a relatively small and static market for managers, especially away from the eastern seaboard. Many senior and middle managers aren't fluent in English. A large number of managers are expatriates. Some members of the Chinese diaspora have returned home to work.
Workers market				
The level of unionization varies among countries. Industrial actions take place in Europe, especially in the manufacturing and public sectors, but not in the United States.	Trade unions are strong and pragmatic, which means that companies can sign agreements with them.	Trade unions are present, but their influence is declining except in certain sectors, such as mining and railways.	The trade union movement is active and volatile, although it is becoming less important. Trade unions have strong political connections.	Workers can join the government-controlled All-China Federation of Trade Unions. Historically, there were no industrial actions, but there have been recent strikes at Hong Kong– and Taiwan-owned manufacturing facilities.

(continued)

Mapping contexts in Brazil, Russia, India, and China (continued)

Capital markets

U.S./EU	Brazil	Russia	India	China
Debt and equity				
Companies can easily get bank loans. The corporate bond market is well developed. The integration of stock exchanges gives companies access to a deep pool of investors.	A good banking system exists, and there is a healthy market for initial public offerings. Wealthy individuals can invest in offshore accounts.	The banking system is strong but dominated by state-owned banks. The consumer credit market is booming, and the IPO market is growing. Firms must incorporate local subsidiaries to raise equity capital.	The local banking system is well developed. Multinationals can rely on local banks for local needs. Equity is available to local and foreign entities.	The local banking system and equity markets are underdeveloped. Foreign companies have to raise both debt and equity in home markets.
Venture capital (VC)				
VC is generally available in urban areas or for specific industry clusters. VC is not as readily available in southern Europe.	A few private equity players are active locally.	Only companies in the most profitable businesses, such as real estate development and natural resources, can access VC.	VC is available in some cities and from the Indian diaspora.	VC availability is limited.

Accounting standards				
Apart from off-balance-sheet items, a high level of transparency exists. In the European Union, accounting practices should become more uniform after 2005 because of new norms.	The financial-reporting system is based on a common-law system and functions well.	The modified Soviet system of financial reporting works well. Banks are shifting to international accounting standards.	Financial reporting, which is based on a common-law system, functions well.	There is little corporate transparency. China's accounting standards are not strict, although the China Securities Regulatory Commission wants to tighten disclosure rules.
Financial distress				
Efficient bankruptcy processes tend to favor certain stakeholders (creditors, labor force, or shareholders) in certain countries.	Processes allow companies to stay in business rather than go out of business. Bankruptcy processes exist but are inefficient.	Bankruptcy processes and legislation are fully developed. Corruption distorts bankruptcy enforcement.	Bankruptcy processes exist but are inefficient. Promoters find it difficult to sell or shut down "sick" enterprises.	Companies can use bankruptcy processes in some cases. Write-offs are common.

Source: Media reports and interviews with academics and businesspeople.

globally competitive. It's difficult to imagine a successful business in China that hasn't had something to do with the government; in India, most companies have succeeded in spite of the state.

Brazil mixes and matches features of both China and India. Like China, Brazil has floated many state-owned enterprises. At the same time, it has kept its doors open to multinationals, and European corporations such as Unilever, Volkswagen, and Nestlé have been able to build big businesses there. Volkswagen has six plants in Brazil, dominates the local market, and exports its Gol model to Argentina and Russia. Brazil also boasts private sector companies that, like Indian firms, go head-to-head in the local market with global firms. Some Brazilian companies, such as basic materials company Votorantim and aircraft maker Embraer, have become globally competitive.

Russia is also a cross between China and India, but most of its companies are less competitive than those in Brazil. A few multinationals such as McDonald's have done well, but most foreign firms have failed to make headway there. There are only a few strong private sector companies in the market, such as dairy products maker Wimm-Bill-Dann and cellular services provider VimpelCom. The Russian government is involved, formally and informally, in several industries. For instance, the government's equity stake in Gazprom allows it to influence the country's energy sector. Moreover, administrators at all levels can exercise near veto power over business deals that involve local or foreign companies, and getting permits and approvals is a complicated chore in Russia.

One level deeper, the financial markets in Brazil, Russia, India, and China vary, too. In Brazil and India, indigenous entrepreneurs, who are multinationals' main rivals, rely on the local capital markets for resources. In China, foreign companies compete with state-owned enterprises, which public sector banks usually fund. The difference is important because neither the Chinese companies nor the banks are under pressure to show profits. Moreover, financial reporting in China isn't transparent even if companies have listed themselves on stock exchanges. State-owned companies can for years pursue strategies that increase their market share at the expense of profits. Corporate governance standards in Brazil and India also mimic those of the West more closely than do those in Russia and China. Thus, in Russia and China, multinationals can't count on local partners' internal systems to protect their interests and assets—especially their intellectual property.

The Three Strategy Choices

When companies tailor strategies to each country's contexts, they can capitalize on the strengths of particular locations. Before adapting their approaches, however, firms must compare the benefits of doing so with the additional coordination costs they'll incur. When they complete this exercise, companies will find that they have three distinct choices: They can adapt their business model to countries while keeping their core value propositions constant, they can try to change the contexts, or they can stay out of countries where adapting strategies may be uneconomical or impractical. Can companies sustain strategies that presume the exis-tence of institutional voids? They can. It took decades to fill institutional voids in the West.

Adapt Your Strategies

To succeed, multinationals must modify their business models for each nation. They may have to adapt to the voids in a country's product markets, its input markets, or both. But companies must retain their core business propositions even as they adapt their business models. If they make shifts that are too radical, these firms will lose their advantages of global scale and global branding.

Compare Dell's business models in the United States and China. In the United States, the hardware maker offers consumers a wide variety of configurations and makes most computers to order. Dell doesn't use distrib-utors or resellers, shipping most machines directly to buyers. In 2003, nearly 50% of the company's revenues in North America came from orders placed through the Internet.

The cornerstone of Dell's business model is that it carries little or no inventory. But Dell realized that its direct-sales approach wouldn't work in China, because individuals weren't accustomed to buying PCs through the Internet. Chinese companies used paper-based order processing, so Dell had to rely on faxes and phones rather than online sales. And several Chinese govern-ment departments and state-owned enterprises insisted that hardware vendors make their bids through systems integrators. The upshot is that Dell relies heavily on distributors and systems integrators in China. When it first entered the market there, the company offered a smaller product range than it did in the United States to keep inventory levels low. Later, as its supply chain became more efficient, it offered customers in China a full range of products.

Smart companies like Dell modify their business model without destroying the parts of it that give them a competitive advantage over rivals. These firms start by identifying the value propositions that they will not modify, whatever the context. That's what McDonald's did even as it comprehensively adapted its business model to Russia's factor markets. In the United States, McDonald's has outsourced most of its supply chain operations. But when it tried to move into Russia in 1990, the company was unable to find local suppliers. The fast-food chain asked several of its European vendors to step up, but they weren't interested. Instead of giving up, McDonald's decided to go it alone. With the help of its joint venture partner, the Moscow City Administration, the company identified some Russian farmers and bakers it could work with. It imported cattle from Holland and russet potatoes from America, brought in agricultural specialists from Canada and Europe to improve the farmers' management practices, and advanced the farmers money so that they could invest in better seeds and equipment.

Then the company built a 100,000 square-foot McComplex in Moscow to produce beef; bakery, potato, and dairy products; ketchup; mustard; and Big Mac sauce. It set up a trucking fleet to move supplies to restaurants and financed its suppliers so that they would have enough working capital to buy modern equipment. The company also brought in about 50 expatriate managers to teach Russian employees about its service standards, quality measurements, and operating procedures and sent a 23-person team of Russian managers to Canada for a four-month training program. McDonald's created a vertically integrated operation in Russia, but the company clung to one principle: It would sell only hamburgers, fries, and Coke to Russians in a clean environment—fast. Fifteen years after serving its first Big Mac in Moscow's Pushkin Square, McDonald's has invested $250 million in the country and controls 80% of the Russian fast-food market.

Change the Contexts

Many multinationals are powerful enough to alter the contexts in which they operate. The products or services these companies offer can force dramatic changes in local markets. When Asia's first satellite TV channel, Hong Kong–based STAR, launched in 1991, for example, it transformed the Indian marketplace in many ways. Not only did the company cause the Indian government to lose its monopoly on television broadcasts overnight, but it also led to a booming TV-manufacturing industry and the launch of several other satellite-based channels aimed at Indian audiences. By the mid-1990s, satellite-based TV channels had become a vibrant advertising medium, and many organizations used them to launch products and services targeted at India's new TV-watching consumer class.

The entry of foreign companies transforms quality standards in local product markets, which can have far-reaching consequences. Japan's Suzuki triggered a quality revolution after it entered India in 1981. The automaker's need for large volumes of high-quality components roused local suppliers. They teamed up with Suzuki's vendors in Japan, formed quality clusters, and worked with Japanese experts to produce better products. During the next two decades, the total quality management movement spread to other industries in India. By 2004, Indian companies had bagged more Deming prizes than firms in any country other than Japan. More important, India's automotive suppliers had succeeded in breaking into the global market, and several of them, such as Sundram Fasteners, had become preferred suppliers to international automakers like GM.

Companies can change contexts in factor markets, too. Consider the capital market in Brazil. As multinationals set up subsidiaries in those countries, they needed global-quality audit services. Few Brazilian accounting firms could provide those services, so the Big Four audit firms—Deloitte Touche Tohmatsu, Ernst & Young, KPMG, and PricewaterhouseCoopers—decided to set up branches there. The presence of those companies quickly raised financial-reporting and auditing standards in Brazil.

In a similar vein, Knauf, one of Europe's leading manufacturers of building materials, is trying to grow Russia's talent market. During the past decade, the German giant has built 20 factories in Russia and invested more than $400 million there. Knauf operates in a people-intensive industry; the company and its subsidiaries have roughly 7,000 employees in Russia. To boost standards in the country's construction industry, Knauf opened an education center in St. Petersburg in 2003 that works closely with the State Architectural and Construction University. The school acts both as a mechanism that supplies talent to Knauf and as an institution that contributes to the much-needed development of Russian architecture.

Indeed, as firms change contexts, they must help countries fully develop their potential. That creates a win-win situation for the country and the company. Metro Cash & Carry, a division of German trading company Metro Group, has changed contexts in a socially beneficial way in several European and Asian countries. The Düsseldorf-based company—which sells everything to restaurants from meats and vegetables to napkins and toothpicks—entered China in 1996, Russia in 2001, and India in 2003. Metro has pioneered business links between farmers and small-scale manufacturers in rural areas that sell their products to small and midsize urban companies.

For instance, Metro invested in a cold chain in China so that it could deliver goods like fish and meats from rural regions to urban locations. That changed local conditions in several important ways. First, Metro's investment induced farmers in China to invest more in their agricultural operations. Metro also lobbied with governments for quality standards to prevent companies from selling shoddy produce to hapless consumers.

By shifting transactions from roadside markets to computerized warehouses, the company's operations brought primary products into the tax net. Governments, which need the money to invest in local services, have remained on the company's side. That's a good thing for Metro since, in developing markets, the jury is always out on foreign companies.

Stay Away

It may be impractical or uneconomical for some firms to adapt their business models to emerging markets. Home Depot, the successful do-it-yourself U.S. retailer, has been cautious about entering developing countries. The company offers a specific value proposition to customers: low prices, great service, and good quality. To pull that off, it relies on a variety of U.S.-specific institutions. It depends on the U.S. highways and logistical management systems to minimize the amount of inventory it has to carry in its large, warehouse-style stores. It relies on employee stock ownership to motivate shop-level workers to render top-notch service. And its value proposition takes advantage of the fact that high labor costs in the United States encourage home owners to engage in do-it-yourself projects.

Home Depot made a tentative foray into emerging markets by setting up two stores in Chile in 1998 and another in Argentina in 2000. In 2001, however, the company sold those operations for a net loss of $14 million. At the time, CEO Robert Nardelli emphasized that most of Home Depot's future growth was likely to come from North America. Despite that initial setback, the company hasn't entirely abandoned emerging markets. Rather, it has switched from a greenfield strategy to an acquisition-led approach. In 2001, Home Depot entered Mexico by buying a home improvement retailer, Total Home, and the next year, it acquired Del Norte, another small chain. By 2004, the company had 42 stores in Mexico. Although Home Depot has recently said that it is exploring the possibility of entering China, perhaps by making an acquisition, it doesn't have retail operations in any other developing countries.

Home Depot must consider whether it can modify its U.S. business model to suit the institutional contexts of emerging markets. In a country with a poorly developed capital market, for example, the company may not be able to use employee stock ownership as a compensation tool. Similarly, in a country with a poorly developed physical infrastructure, Home Depot may have difficulty using its inventory management systems, a scenario that would alter the economics of the business. In markets where labor costs are relatively low, the target customer may not be the home owner but rather contractors who serve as intermediaries between the store and the home owner. That change in customer focus may warrant an entirely different marketing and merchandising strategy—one that Home Depot isn't convinced it should deploy yet.

While companies can't use the same strategies in all developing countries, they can generate synergies by treating different markets as part of a system. For instance, GE Healthcare (formerly GE Medical Systems) makes parts for its diagnostic machines in China, Hungary, and Mexico and develops the software for those machines in India. The company created this system when it realized that the market for diagnostic machines was small in most low-income countries. GE Healthcare then decided to use the facility it had set up in India in 1990 as a global sourcing base. After several years, and on the back of borrowed expertise from GE Japan, the India operation's products finally met GE Healthcare's exacting standards. In the late 1990s, when GE Healthcare wanted to move a plant from Belgium to cut costs, the Indian subsidiary beat its Mexican counterpart by delivering the highest quality at the lowest cost. Under its then-CEO, Jeff Immelt, GE Healthcare learned to use all its operations in low-income countries—China, Hungary, Mexico, and India— as parts of a system that allowed the company to produce equipment cheaply for the world market.

Parent company GE has also tapped into the talent pool in emerging markets by setting up technology centers in Shanghai and Bangalore, for instance. In those centers, the company conducts research on everything from materials design to molecular modeling to power electronics. GE doesn't treat China and India just as markets but also as sources of talent and innovation that can transform its value chain. And that's how multinational companies should engage with emerging markets if they wish to secure their future.

Note

Andy Klump, Niraj Kaji, Luis Sanchez, and Max Yacoub provided research assistance for the Dell and McDonald's examples in this article.

TARUN KHANNA is the Jorge Paulo Lemann Professor and **KRISHNA G. PALEPU** is the Ross Graham Walker Professor of Business Administration at Harvard Business School. **JAYANT SINHA** is a partner at McKinsey & Company in New Delhi.

Originally published in June 2005. Reprint R0506C

The Hidden Risks in Emerging Markets

by Witold J. Henisz and Bennet A. Zelner

WHEN A FIRM WITH a value-generating technological or managerial capability invests abroad, its shareholders and the host country's citizens both stand to benefit. But no matter how good the apparent fit between what foreign companies offer and what host countries need, success is far from assured. Elections and other political events, economic crises, and changing societal attitudes can disrupt the best-laid plans in both emerging and advanced economies. The interplay of these forces—and the implications for the political choices that multinational firms make—will become especially prominent as national governments chart an uncertain course toward stabilization following the global financial meltdown.

Issues such as taxation of executive compensation, the proper scope of financial regulation, and international M&A have come to the foreground in the wake of the crisis, and stark international differences in opinions and policies on these matters are already evident. The differences will only become more pronounced as discussions about the appropriate near-term policy response to the crisis give way to debates about who should pay and how much. Politicians will struggle to balance popular demands to punish those perceived as responsible against fears of stymied innovation and the flight of human and financial capital. Broader domestic economic concerns—for example, protectionist sentiment in response to the realignment of economic power in favor of emerging nations such as China and India—will inevitably affect the debate as well. The multinational firms best able to anticipate and manage the related risks and opportunities will have the strongest competitive edge.

Historically, the biggest risks faced by foreign investors were in developing countries with immature or volatile political systems. The chief concern was "expropriation risk," the possibility that host governments would seize foreign-owned assets. Today, this risk has largely disappeared. Stronger international law and the symbiotic nature of growth in emerging and developed economies reduced asset seizures to nearly zero during the 1980s. However, as interest in emerging markets has soared, host countries have learned, according to George Chifor at the University of Windsor in Canada, "that more value can be extracted from foreign enterprises through the more subtle instrument of regulatory control rather than outright seizures." The risk that a government will discriminatorily change the laws, regulations, or contracts governing an investment—or

Idea in Brief

You may think that the biggest political risk to your assets in a developing country is outright seizure by its government. Not so. Other, less overt policy weapons have become the main threats, and it takes political deftness to anticipate and outwit the players who wield them. Wharton's Witold J. Henisz and Duke's Bennet A. Zelner discuss the tools, both human and technological, that businesses can use to outmaneuver the forces that put their foreign profits at risk. They also share success stories of companies such as the Italian oil giant Eni, which has managed overseas risk by balancing operational efficiency with political capital, mastering the art of political spin, and hitting the pressure points of local stakeholders. Together, the authors' insights constitute a set of best-practice guidelines for assessing the landscape abroad and for modeling political decision making.

will fail to enforce them—in a way that reduces an investor's financial returns is what we call "policy risk."

Although the data on policy risk are less clear-cut than the hard numbers on direct seizures, press mentions of policy risk (using terms such as "political risk," "political uncertainty," "policy risk," "policy uncertainty," "regulatory risk," and "regulatory uncertainty") indicate that it has risen dramatically as seizure risk has fallen. (See the exhibit "The changing face of risk in emerging markets.") Press mentions of actual seizures have also increased somewhat since 2001, but that does not reflect a broad-based resurgence in seizures.

Other recent data are consistent with the finding that policy risk has increased greatly. A 2001 Price-WaterhouseCoopers study concluded that an opaque policy-making environment is equivalent to at least a 33% increase in taxation. A World Bank study in 2004

The changing face of risk in emerging markets

Overt seizures of foreign assets by host countries in emerging markets essentially evaporated by 1980. However, other political risks to those assets (for example, from potential regulatory action) have risen dramatically since then.

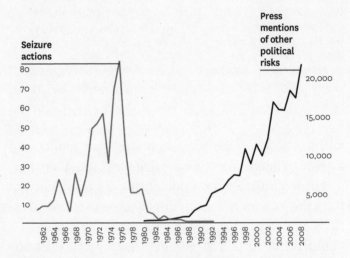

Source: Seizure data (left side) from M.S. Minor, "The Demise of Expropriation as an Instrument of LDC Policy, 1980–1992," *Journal of International Business Studies* 25 (1994): 177–88.

revealed that 15% to 30% of the contracts covering $371 billion of private infrastructure investment in the 1990s were subject to government-initiated renegotiations or disputes. And a 2009 survey by the Multilateral Investment Guarantee Agency and the Economist Intelligence Unit found that multinational enterprises considered breach of contract, restrictions on the transfer and convertibility of profits, civil disturbance, government failure to honor guarantees, and regulatory restrictions all to be more significant risks than the potential seizure of assets.

Unfortunately, the traditional financial and contractual mechanisms that firms use to assess and mitigate business risks have limited value. Therefore, investors must develop proactive political-management strategies that lessen government officials' incentives to divert investors' returns. In this article, we explore the experiences of multinational investors as they confront these issues in a variety of industries and countries, and we offer best-practice guidelines for assessing the political landscape and for modeling political decision making. As with the management of any risk or uncertainty, political mastery can become a source of competitive advantage in addition to a means of avoiding losses.

It's Hard to Hedge Policy Risk

Firms engaged in international business often use some combination of legal contracts, insurance, and trade in financial instruments to protect the income streams from their investments against currency or price swings. These approaches, however, offer little protection against policy risk.

For starters, legal contracts are useful only if they are enforced, and shifting laws and regulations can render them void. In the 1990s many Southeast Asian governments wooing private power investors offered contracts that insulated the investors from risks related to lower-than-expected demand, fuel supplies, exchange rates, currency conversions, regulations, and political force majeure. The Asian financial crisis in 1997 brought those investors' favorable treatment into sharp relief as currency values, share prices, and electricity demand all plummeted. Political officials had to choose between honoring the contracts, at the risk of compromising their own popular support, and renegotiating them in order to maintain that support. In the end, many career-minded public officials in Southeast Asia chose to renegotiate or cancel scores of contracts.

Even when contracts can be legally enforced, experience shows that inventive politicians can circumvent them, through a wide variety of means other than changing laws. For example, in 1998, when U.S.-based AES Corporation—then the world's largest independent power company—acquired the Georgian electricity distribution company Telasi, high-priced lawyers constructed an ironclad set of guarantees that allowed AES-Telasi to pass the costs of policy and other risks on to Georgian consumers. One analyst remarked to us, "If you believed the contract, AES was guaranteed a 20% return on its investment." The Georgian government actually never interfered formally with AES-Telasi's ability to pass costs on to consumers. However, the venture was doomed by public officials' inaction—for instance, their failure to terminate supply to nonpaying industrial consumers, to supply fuel to AES-Telasi, and to keep the government's own account current—and by the government's demand for tax payments on electricity for which the company had never been paid. The result was that AES's "guaranteed" 20% return became a shareholder loss of $300 million.

Insurance offers limited protection against policy risk because a firm's exposure is largely determined by its own ability to manage the policy-making process. In the words of one insurer: "I prefer to focus on what my assured [customer] can bring to a risk. My reasoning is that if you back the right assured, you can usually keep problems from occurring in the first place—and if they do happen, you have an excellent chance of mitigating your loss." Yet it is very difficult for insurers to know who the "right assured" is, and the firms with the greatest risk exposure are often those most likely to seek insurance in the first place. As a result, underwriters price their products extremely high, offer very short-term coverage, or don't offer any coverage at all.

Financial hedges have limited value for similar reasons. Instruments for hedging against risks in specific emerging markets—such as exchange-rate, market, and credit risks—are ubiquitous because multiple parties are willing to participate. The project- and firm-specific nature of policy risk, however, renders conventional hedging strategies infeasible.

Some of the more-inventive instruments are based on the average risk premium associated with existing companies in a given country—but they give false comfort. Because the baseline risk premiums are those of firms that are actively participating in a given market (and that often have their risk-mitigation strategies in place), new entrants are likely to face far greater exposure. In fact, foreign investors who focus on constructing financial hedges at the expense of developing their own risk-mitigation strategies may increase their exposure. It is therefore not surprising that, despite the ability to calculate residual risk premiums, no financial institutions have used such premiums to price an instrument that pays out money when a policy risk is realized.

The New Risk-Management Playbook

Given the difficulty of constructing hedges against policy risk through contracts, insurance, or financial risk-management tools, foreign investors must accept the responsibility for directly managing the risk themselves. For many companies, that means rewriting the playbook. Instead of looking for immediate ways to improve operations, managers have to move beyond the quick cost-benefit analyses that they usually undertake and think more about how they can frame and shape public debate. And they must learn how to apply political pressure, either individually or as part of a coalition.

Investing in Goodwill

In the developed world, managers spend a great deal of time and energy on improving efficiency. When companies move into less developed markets, they often expect huge, instant efficiency gains from exploiting the technologies, business models, and practices that they have managed to hone in their home markets. Unfortunately, the political costs of such practices may outweigh those gains.

Consider the 1997 Christmas blackout in large parts of Brazil, including Rio de Janeiro. The then recently privatized electric utility Light (in which AES held a 13.75% stake) faced record-high outdoor temperatures that week, and it was already struggling with poorly maintained equipment that had deteriorated before privatization. However, the press and the public focused on the 40% reduction in personnel, combined with the utility company's record profits, to paint a picture of an exploitative foreign investor. The negative sentiment toward foreign firms in general and AES in particular contributed to the awarding of a 900-megawatt energy-supply contract the following spring to a joint venture led by Brazilian firms (Votorantim Group, Bradesco Group, and Camargo Corrêa) rather than consortia led by AES and British Gas.

A smarter approach was used by Italian state-owned oil company Eni. After the 1998 devaluation of the *real*, when many companies put their investment plans on hold or even exited Brazil, Eni's then-CEO, Franco Bernabe, visited Rio de Janeiro to announce a $500 million investment. He proclaimed: "Now is the time to show that Petrobras [the state-owned oil company] has long-term friends." Eni and Petrobras have collaborated closely ever since.

Framing the Debate

When companies enter new countries, they often engage in extensive PR campaigns that amount to little more than advertisements for the brand and specific commercial ventures. Instead, firms need to master the art of political spin. Presenting a venture as "fair," "equitable," or "growth enhancing" is often a simpler and more powerful means of securing political support than providing a cost-benefit analysis. The precise meaning attributed to such labels varies depending on a firm's market position. New entrants garner support for policies that favor them over incumbents by citing the abuse of monopoly power. Conversely, dominant firms appeal to "fairness" by arguing that smaller entrants cannot survive without the government's helping hand.

This type of debate played out in the South Korean wireless market. LG Telecom—the third entrant, behind the much larger SK Telecom and Korea Telecom—made repeated calls for "asymmetric" government regulation of the market leaders in order to "level the playing field." As the *Korea Times* reported, "The defining question is whether the government will back new entrants in the name of encouraging fair competition, or limit the pool to experienced players." LG ultimately prevailed: In May 2001 the South Korean government announced that it would "guarantee a market share of at least 20% for a third major telecom operator through asymmetric regulation on Korea Telecom and SK Telecom."

Finding Political Pressure Points

The network of relationships in a society greatly influences policy outcomes, especially in countries with weak legal systems. To turn these networks to their advantage, international investors must identify and engage local politicians' power bases. Once again, Eni has shown the way, this time in Kazakhstan. Through its subsidiary Agip KCO, Eni has adopted a business model that responds to the former Soviet republic's economic and social needs. The company favors Kazakh over non-Kazakh suppliers, and it conducts knowledge-transfer, training, and development seminars for them. At least 60% of local employees are Kazakh citizens. The company also funds the construction of various public works, including the national library, the prime minister's residence, schools, computer labs, and multifamily housing units for the poor. As a result, many Kazakh officials now have a stake in Eni's success.

For the vast majority of organizations—which do not possess enough leverage to influence the full range of relevant actors on their own—a crucial component of an effective strategy is to assemble a coalition of interests. In the South Korean wireless battle, LG Telecom benefited from the influence of upstream suppliers. The major Korean carriers wanted to shift to the globally favored WCDMA standard for the newest generation of cellular service, but domestic champion Samsung had developed a global leadership position in the competing CDMA2000 technology. Under pressure from Samsung, the government insisted that one of the new 3G licenses be awarded to LG Telecom in return for its promise to adopt CDMA2000.

An international investor's home government can also be a powerful channel of influence. Observers in central Europe have noted the lobbying success of the German and French governments on behalf of national champions in countries seeking EU membership. However, the use of "foreign influence" may create a perception of meddling, can stoke nationalism, and is generally less likely to have a lasting impact. There's also the risk that your home government will sacrifice your needs in order to gain traction on another issue.

Taking these pages out of the political playbook requires building the sorts of capabilities in intelligence gathering and analysis that are familiar to politicians, spies, and journalists. Managers must begin by understanding the attitudes, opinions, and positions of relevant actors toward their firm, the industry in which the firm operates, and any specific actions that the firm might take to influence outcomes on the playing field.

Tapping the Right Flow of Data

Traditionally, managers who have undertaken political analyses in a host country have directly consulted employees, local business partners, and supply chain partners. The information-gathering process varies in intensity and structure, ranging from surveying radio and newspaper stories to conversing with locals to using computerized contact-management systems. Some firms rely almost exclusively on informal chats, whereas others favor more-formal Delphi (iterative expert survey) methods. (Also see the sidebar "Why Country Risk Ratings Don't Work.")

Although these sources provide valuable conventional input, they can require more time and money than such small, subjective, potentially biased snapshots might merit. Moreover, given the availability of multiple real-time indicators and metrics in functional areas such as finance, marketing, and human resources, CEOs and boards of directors increasingly demand similar real-time data on the preferences of key players. This human intelligence can be effectively and continuously incorporated into enterprise risk-management models and frameworks.

To broaden their perspectives, more and more companies are reaching out to nonbusiness organizations that can help them anticipate and preempt consumer concerns about environmental, health, and safety issues. For example, after a bruising experience over the disposal of its Brent Spar oil-drilling platform in 1995, Royal Dutch Shell now routinely includes Greenpeace in substantive environmental discussions. Some companies also consult professional experts, ranging from well-positioned ex-government officials operating on retainer; to the stringers who write for the Economist Intelligence Unit, Stratfor, and Oxford Analytica; to global political consultancies, such as Political Risk Services or Eurasia Group. Although employees, suppliers, and activists may have access to better information, they lack the specialized training that these advisers bring to the table.

Of increasing importance is the vast amount of information emanating from third-party sources—primarily the mainstream news media, but also bloggers and other observers—that routinely monitor the policy-making process in various countries. The large volume and relatively unfocused nature of the material make it hard to synthesize, digest, and act upon effectively, even if

Why Country Risk Ratings Don't Work

WHEN IT COMES TO ASSESSING LEVELS of policy risk, managers are far too quick to rely on the subjective ratings of country "experts." One popular index focuses on asset-seizure and contract-repudiation risks. Ratings are incorporated, in the form of country risk premiums, into the discount rates used to evaluate investment opportunities. This approach appears to have the formal rigor of financial risk management, but it is actually inadequate.

To begin with, such ratings usually fail to account for the fact that the levels of policy risk vary among different investors in a country, some of whom may adapt their business practices to local norms and lobby key policy makers better than others do. Also, policy-risk exposure is to some extent contingent on the relative importance of the proposed investment to the two parties (how easy is it for the firm to walk away, and how badly does the local government want the deal?). Finally, country risk ratings are usually retrospective, reflecting past policy outcomes. To assess the correlation with current policy risk, an analyst needs to determine how similar the past and present policy-shaping factors actually are.

---

a company has substantial resources for this activity. However, with information-extraction software, it's now possible to identify the relevant political and social actors on a given issue and their intensity of interest in it.

One approach, known as data mining, relies on the coincident location of words to derive information about key players' preferences. For example, the occurrence of "Russia," "AES-Telasi," and "protest" in the same sentence implies a negative sentiment in the relationship between Russia and the electricity investor

Even as purely country-level measures, most political risk score-cards are woefully short on analysis, as an example from Chile and Indonesia clearly shows. In 1997, one risk index ascribed an identical score to those two countries. The measure took no account of the significant institutional differences between them. Faced with violent citizen demands to redistribute investor returns in the wake of the 1997 Asian financial crisis, Indonesia's longtime military dictator, General Suharto, renegotiated contracts with foreign investors that were unaffiliated with his family or close friends. After he was ousted in a coup, the previously favored companies experienced a backlash as the successor government renegotiated their contracts.

Chile, in contrast, had a democratic multiparty system and possessed a well-respected independent judiciary—a further check against arbitrary policy change. Pressures in Chile to enhance equity and social cohesion culminated in the 2000 election of socialist Ricardo Lagos as president. He shifted some discretionary spending toward social programs but also respected the rule of law and existing commercial contracts. Underlying risks in Chile and Indonesia were therefore very different, but the country-level ratings didn't reflect those distinct realities.

AES-Telasi. Another tool, called natural language parsing (NLP) software, facilitates more-refined sentence-level inferences by syntactically distinguishing among subjects, verbs, and objects, thereby identifying the orientation of actions or preferences. Consider this possible sentence: "The Union of Consumers of Georgia is outraged by the AES-Telasi American company proposal to increase the tariff on electric energy." NLP software would recognize the precise grammatical relationship among "Union of Consumers of Georgia," "is outraged

Are the locals hostile to you?

Information-extraction software can capture changes in attitudes toward a business venture by syntactically analyzing the content of media reports about it. This example compares the total number of sentences in articles about Gabriel Resources' plan to develop the Rosia Montana gold mine in Romania with the percentage of sentences indicating NGO opposition to the plan.

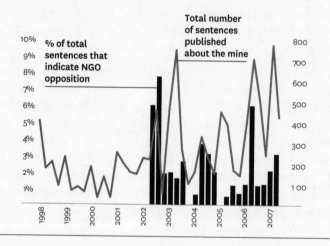

by," and "AES-Telasi . . . proposal"—pointing to a strong negative sentiment toward the U.S. company. NLP software can also gauge the intensity of sentiment. If the verb phrase in the sentence had been "objects to" instead of "is outraged by," the software would have recognized that the sentiment of the Union of Consumers of Georgia toward AES was negative, but less so.

Similarly, information-extraction tools can readily and objectively highlight shifts in an actor's preferences over time. For example, a coalition of local and international activists sharply contested the plan by Canadian mining company Gabriel Resources to develop the Rosia Montana gold mine in Romania. The exhibit "Are the Locals Hostile to You?" plots the frequency in the worldwide media of sentences mentioning statements or actions against the mine by nongovernmental organizations through 2007, relative to the total number of sentences in articles about the mine during the same period. The data show that NGOs were relatively indifferent to the issue until mid-2002, when negative reports increased sharply.

The "Tummy Test" and Other Models

With data about political actors and their level of interest in hand, managers must then synthesize that information into a model of the policy-making process. At the informal end of the synthesis spectrum is the "tummy test," in which a decision maker who has spoken with or been briefed about relevant sources draws upon his or her own knowledge of similar cases to make an educated guess about the likely policy outcome. The accuracy of this technique clearly varies enormously according to the skill set of the decision maker and the relevance of his or her past experience to the current situation. To improve the accuracy of such judgments, managers can also involve specialized consultancies that draw upon a more diverse set of experiences from multiple firms and industries in the target country or a comparable one.

A sophisticated extension of the tummy test is the "war room," in which managers come together for a one-off meeting or a series of brainstorming sessions. Sessions may be scheduled regularly or triggered by a shock or event that requires a strategic response. "Influence maps" are used to depict each politically relevant actor as a bubble arrayed in space according to the player's position on a given issue, with the size of the bubble proportional to the player's power. Linkages across actors or clusters of actors can be indicated by either location or connecting lines. Although no formal analytic tools are used, the maps can help guide discussion of action scenarios: What happens if we target actor X? What if we break the link between X and Y? What if we try to reduce Z's power? The insights produced by this approach are, of course, only as good as the information brought into the room and the quality of the team assembled.

The most formal tool for modeling the policymaking process is the dynamic expected utility model, which is based on game theory. It assumes that, in each of several time periods, every actor (an individual or an organization) with a vested interest in an issue has a choice of three possible alternatives: proposing a policy, opposing a proposed policy, or doing nothing. Each actor chooses the alternative that maximizes his, her, or its expected utility in each period. The selection depends on the direction and intensity of the actor's preferences, the salience of the issue, the cost of proposing or opposing a policy, and similar information about other actors. The combined actions of all the actors result in a likely policy outcome. The sensitivity of the outcome to various assumptions and parameters can then be calculated, helping to identify which actors are so pivotal that a change in their preferences, power, or salience would have a large impact on policy.

Models like this are widely used by the intelligence community and by specialist consulting groups such as Mesquita & Roundell, Sentia Group, the Probity Group, and Commetrix. A growing number of multinational corporations are also adopting these tools. A large British company, for example, used such a model to decide how to influence the climate change debate in the European Union. Analysts first identified which actors were most commonly cited in the press and whom these actors referenced in their speeches and writings. The analysts then constructed a network of key "influencers" and modeled various points of entry into this system to identify the target areas and the messages that would maximize their effect on the climate change debate.

Although the integration of automated data collection, dynamic expected utility modeling, and influence-map visualizations remains in its infancy, the potential applications are broader than the management of policy risk alone. Marketing research, financial analysis, operations, and human resources all could benefit from a richer analysis of the best ways to affect stakeholders' opinions.

Of course, the risks of investment may simply be too great to justify entry into certain political zones. But in many cases investors who explicitly recognize the dynamism of the environment and implement appropriate strategies to address it will find the risks quite manageable. By combining data-mining and modeling technologies with traditional approaches, as we've described, they can start the journey forward, moving from "tummy tests" toward an analytically oriented, defensible system for managing policy risk that will greatly expand their investment options. At its heart, this system will always retain elements of tacit knowledge and experience, and not all managers and firms will be able to master its intricacies. But those that do will find it a powerful source of competitive advantage.

WITOLD J. HENISZ is a professor at the University of Pennsylvania's Wharton School. **BENNET A. ZELNER** is a professor at Duke University's Fuqua School of Business.

Originally published in April 2010. Reprint R1004H

Managing Risk in an Unstable World

by Ian Bremmer

COUNTRIES IN TURMOIL ELBOW one another off the front page at a dizzying pace: Lebanon follows Ukraine follows Sudan follows Argentina. Companies, meanwhile, fear unpredictable change, even as they seek profit from the opportunities change creates—a freshly privatized industry in Turkey, recently tendered oil blocks in Libya, a new pro-Western government in the former Soviet republic of Ukraine. To help weigh dangers against opportunities, corporations mulling foreign ventures routinely consult economic risk analysts. But basing global investment decisions on economic data without understanding the political context is like basing nutrition decisions on calorie counts without examining the list of ingredients.

Reassuring data on countries' per capita income, growth, and inflation—the bread and butter of economic risk analysis—often obscures potential threats from other sources. Iran's parliament, for example, last year passed legislation that complicates foreign companies' abilities to plant stakes in that country's telecom sector. The 2003 revolution in Georgia altered the strategic calculus for investment in Caspian Sea energy development. The Kremlin's politically motivated prosecution of business tycoon Mikhail Khodorkovsky sent a chill through Russia's oil market. And Brazil's government is pressing both its agencies and its citizens to adopt open-source software, a policy that could inflict some nasty wounds on Microsoft and other technology companies.

These are examples of *political risk,* broadly defined as the impact of politics on markets. Political risk is influenced by the passage of laws, the foibles of leaders, and the rise of popular movements—in short, all the factors that might politically stabilize or destabilize a country. The significance of any given risk, of course, depends upon the context of the investment decision. A hedge fund manager worries about developments that could move markets tomorrow, while the leader of a corporation building an overseas chemical plant needs a longer view. Strategists evaluating emerging markets must be especially vigilant (in fact, an emerging market may be defined as a state in which politics matters at least as much as economics). But even those businesses active only in developed nations should factor political risk into their planning scenarios.

Most companies are already navigating the choppy waters of globalization, and none, presumably, are sailing blind. But corporate leaders may lack the sophisticated understanding this very complex subject requires. Political risk analysis is more subjective than its economic counterpart and demands that leaders grapple

Idea in Brief

To navigate globalization's choppy waters, every business leader analyzes economic risk when considering overseas investments. But do you also look *beyond* reassuring data about per-capita income or economic growth—to assess the **political risk** of doing business in particular countries? If not, you may get blindsided when political forces reshape markets in unexpected ways. Iran's parliament, for instance, passed legislation in 2004 complicating foreign companies' ability to plant stakes in that country's telecom sector.

Appraising the myriad shifting political influences on your global investments isn't easy—because political risk is hard to quantify. For example, how do you measure the impact of a national leader's personality quirks on his country's economic landscape?

Your strategy? In addition to analyzing economic risk, assess the four dimensions of political risk: Examine the stability and strength of **government** in nations where you're exposed. Assess **social trends** such as growing income gaps and unemployment levels. Evaluate **security** by discerning how prepared a country is for natural disasters. And consider **economic factors,** such as a nation's debt and openness to foreign investment.

By blending political and economic risk analysis, you make savvier investment decisions—seizing valuable opportunities around the globe while avoiding danger zones.

not just with broad, easily observable trends but also with nuances of society and even quirks of personality. And those hard-to-quantify factors must constantly be pieced into an ongoing narrative within historical and regional contexts.

This article will help corporate leaders become better appraisers of information about the myriad shifting influences on global investments. Armed with that

Idea in Practice

To minimize risk in your overseas investments, assess the following dimensions of political risk.

Government

How strong are the government and the rule of law? Early in 2005, for example, Turkey's government was powerful and cohesive, and had gained popularity thanks to economic recovery and the European Union's decision to open membership talks to Turkey. These developments indicate a relatively high level of political stability.

Also consider the level of corruption in government. You'll need proxy metrics: For example, to evaluate the integrity of a country's judiciary, ask, Are judges paid a living wage? Do programs exist to inform them about new legislation? Are judges often targeted for assassination?

Society

How much social tension exists? How disaffected are the nation's youth? How secure do individuals feel? To find clues, study the percentage of children who regularly attend school. Compare police and military salaries relative to criminal income opportunities. Assess young people's access to medical care, unemployment rates, and imprisonment rates.

Persistent or widening socioeconomic inequalities—such as those in Turkey—can also signal possible social unrest leading to political instability.

Security

How stable are the country's geopolitical alliances? How prepared is the nation for emergencies, natural disasters, and internal strife?

understanding, business strategists can minimize risks and seize opportunities far beyond their home shores.

Politics Is Everyone's Business

Corporations with investments in such opaque countries as Zimbabwe, Myanmar, and Vietnam have long understood how political risk affects their bottom lines.

Example: Turkey's security has come into question, owing to the continued presence of Kurdistan Workers' Party militants in northern Iraq. The Turkish government worries that Kurds—empowered by the Iraqi elections—may seek to regain control of the oil-rich northern Iraqi town of Kirkuk. This could provide the financial basis for an independent Kurdish state near Turkey's border—which in turn could fan separatist flames in Turkey's own Kurdish population. Turkey's concerns over growing Kurdish strength in Iraq have also strained its traditionally close ties with the United States—suggesting potential obstacles to American investments in that country.

Economic

What are the country's fiscal position, growth and investment, and debt? How economically open is the country? Does its political openness match its economic openness? If not, instability may ensue.

Example: Economically, China is opening rapidly—as diplomats and negotiators globe trot in search of new trade relationships to feed the country's growth. But China is still politically closed: This police state exerts absolute control over public expression. It's also marked by corruption and inefficiency. Simultaneously, reforms are straining relationships between national and regional leaders, increasing the probability of an economic shock—followed by a political one.

In fact, historically, some of the business world's best political risk analysis has come from multinational corporations, like Royal Dutch/Shell and American International Group (AIG), that have entire departments dedicated to the subject. But today, any company with exposure in foreign markets needs early, accurate information on political developments. There are four principle reasons for this.

First, international markets are more interconnected than ever before. Tremors following a market shock in Argentina are quickly felt in Brazil and Venezuela, but they also rumble through Thailand. In 1997, capital flight from Southeast Asia roiled markets around the world. If China's rapidly growing economy overshoots a soft landing and crashes into recession, the impact on Chile, Russia, India, and the United States will be measurable within hours. China's political decisions today will have dramatic long-term effects on its markets. Companies with exposure anywhere in the world that China does business ignore those decisions at their peril.

Second, for good or ill, the United States is making the world a more volatile place, and that has changed risk calculations everywhere. The attacks on the World Trade Center in New York put foreign affairs and security front and center of federal government policy. Washington has shown its willingness to aggressively preempt threats to American security and national interests. The U.S. military has demonstrated an unprecedented capability to respond to international shocks—and to create them.

Third, the offshoring trend is growing. Businesses shift some operations to countries where labor is cheap—but the labor is cheap for a reason. In countries such as India (an established offshoring destination) and Kenya (an emerging one), living conditions for the working classes can be harsh, and there is greater threat of unrest than in developed countries with their large, relatively prosperous middle classes. Offshoring presents other risks as well. The Chinese government, for example, is already cavalier about intellectual property rights and shows signs of becoming more so. Companies moving manufacturing and other functions there may be hard-pressed to protect some of their most valuable intellectual assets.

Fourth, the world is increasingly dependent for energy on states troubled by considerable political risk—Saudi Arabia, Iran, Nigeria, Russia, and Venezuela among them. As global supply struggles to keep pace with rising demand, political instability in these oil-producing states can quickly produce shocks all over the world.

It is difficult to imagine a business that is not affected by at least one or two of these developments. And corporations' exposure will only grow as supply chains become more global and developing countries increasingly participate in international trade.

What Economics Can't Tell You

Economic risk analysis and political risk analysis address two fundamentally different questions. Economic risk analysis tells corporate leaders whether a particular country *can* pay its debt. Political risk analysis tells them whether that country *will* pay its debt. Two examples illustrate this distinction.

When 35-year-old Sergei Kiriyenko replaced Viktor Chernomyrdin as prime minister in March 1998, Russia's economy seemed to be emerging from post–Soviet era turmoil. Inflation had been reduced to single digits, the economy was growing, and the government appeared committed to a moderate reformist path. Economic analysts saw clear skies.

But political analysts recognized that an obstructionist parliament intended to block Kremlin attempts to tighten fiscal policy and streamline tax collection. They saw that an absence of consensus was producing incoherent monetary policies and that the absentee, alcoholic president wasn't going to enforce discipline on an increasingly chaotic policy-formulation process. When oil prices fell, political analysts underlined the country's lack of fiscal discipline as a cause for immediate concern.

In short, political analysts produced a darker—and more accurate—portrait of Russia's market instability in the period leading up to the financial crisis of 1998. When Russia ultimately defaulted on international debt and devalued the ruble, companies that had studied both economic and political risk weathered the storm with far fewer repercussions than those that had relied on economic analysis alone.

In other instances, political risk analysts have been able to detect the silver linings in economists' dark clouds. The value of Brazilian bonds and currency fell sharply in 2002 when it became clear that Luis Inacio Lula da Silva would be elected that country's president. In earlier campaigns, Lula had criticized the International Monetary Fund and Brazil's fiscal conservatives, whom he accused of widening the gap between rich and poor. Comparisons of Lula with Cuba's Fidel Castro and Venezuelan president Hugo Chávez spooked economic risk analysts, who feared that the election of Brazil's first "leftist" president would produce a politically driven market crisis.

But many political analysts considered such an outcome unlikely. In Lula they saw not an ideologue or a theoretician but a man who made his name as a tough, pragmatic labor negotiator. They observed in his campaign an inclusive, conciliatory electoral strategy. They heard in his speeches a determination not to allow Brazil to fall into the kind of financial crisis that had inflicted so much damage on Argentina. And so they argued that Lula's victory would be more likely to produce political and economic stability. If Lula won, they predicted, his government would enfranchise the poor. And he would keep his campaign promise to reserve an IMF-established percentage of tax revenue for the repayment of debt, instead of spending it on social programs and make-work projects.

The political analysts were right. Lula won the election and kept his promises of fiscal discipline. Within weeks, Brazilian bonds staged a dramatic recovery.

Strength Against Shocks

In both Russia and Brazil, political analysts focused on how a specific leadership change would affect the country's *stability*—the unit of measure for political risk. A nation's stability is determined by two things: political leaders' capacity to implement the policies they want even amidst shocks and their ability to avoid generating shocks of their own. A country with both capabilities will always be more stable than a country with just one. Countries with neither are the most vulnerable to political risk.

Shocks themselves are another important concept in political risk. They can be either internal (demonstrations in Egypt; a transfer of political power in Cuba) or external (thousands of refugees fleeing from North Korea into China; the tsunami in Southeast Asia). The presence of shocks alone, however, is not a sign of instability. Saudi Arabia, for example, has produced countless shocks over the years but has so far ridden out the tremors. It will probably continue to do so, at least in the near term: The nation is built on political and religious fault lines, but its strong authoritarian control and deep pockets allow the Saudi elite to adapt to quite dramatic changes.

Saudi Arabia's relative stability is grounded in its capacity to withstand shocks; other countries depend more on their capacity not to produce them. Kazakhstan's political structure, for example, is less supple and adaptable than that of Saudi Arabia. But the country also stands much further from the epicenter of political earthquakes.

Clearly then, two countries will react differently to similar shocks, depending on how stable they are. Say an election is held and a head of state is chosen but the victory is challenged by a large number of voters, and the nation's highest judicial body must rule on a recount. That happened in the United States in 2000 without any significant implications for the stability of the country or its markets. When similar events erupted in Taiwan in 2003 and Ukraine in 2004, however, demonstrations closed city streets, civil violence threatened, and international observers speculated on the viability of those nations' economies.

The 2000 U.S. elections point to another complicating factor in political risk: the relationship between stability and openness. The United States is stable because it is open—information flows widely, people express themselves freely, and institutions matter more than personalities. Consequently, the nation weathered its election controversy without a Wall Street panic; investors knew the problem would be resolved and that the outcome would be broadly perceived as legitimate.

But other countries—such as North Korea, Myanmar, and Cuba—are stable because they are closed. What's more, the slightest opening could push the most brittle of these nations into dangerous territory. Twenty minutes' exposure to CNN would reveal to North Korean citizens how outrageously their government lies to them about life outside; the result might be significant unrest. And while there is considerable world pressure on closed countries to open up, the transition from a stable-because-closed state to a stable-because-open state is inevitably marked by instability. Some nations, for instance South Africa, survive that transition. Others, like the Soviet Union, collapse.

Plotting where nations lie on the openness-stability spectrum, and in which direction they are heading, is tricky. And no country poses a greater challenge than China, which appears equally at home on two different

Why China Keeps Us Up at Night

CHINA BESTRIDES THE WORLD of political risk like a colossus. Many experts tout it as the great investment opportunity of the new millennium, but it is also a great unknown. Among the questions political risk analysts are studying: Can China's explosive economic growth survive its corrupt and inefficient political system? Do the country's political leaders agree that preparations for a soft landing to avoid recession are necessary? Would reform that opens its political process make China more stable or less?

China's continued expansion depends on the central government's capacity to handle complex economic transitions and avoid instability. At the same time, the state must juggle huge security, demographic, and political challenges. Imminent agricultural, banking, and urban policy reforms will probably produce even more complex management problems for the country's dysfunctional bureaucracy.

China appears to be inching toward instability as reforms strain the relationships between national and regional leaders, increasing the probability of an economic shock followed by a political one. Complicating matters, China's bureaucracy lacks the admin-

points along this range. Politically, China is stable-because-closed; it is a police state with absolute control over public expression. For example, security forces severely restricted media coverage of the recent death of Zhao Ziyang, a relatively progressive politician, in order to prevent the kinds of uprisings sparked by the deaths of Chou En-lai in 1976 and Hu Yaobang in 1989. Economically, however, China is opening at a rapid clip, as diplomats and negotiators globe trot in search of new trade relationships to feed the country's growth.

When a country is politically closed but economically open, something has to give. Whether China's political istrative control necessary to modulate the pace of an economic slowdown.

Analysts of economic risk tend to base projections for China's growth rates on its past performance. But there are few countries for which past performance is so poor a predictor of future results. With a few notable exceptions, such as the 1989 protests in Tiananmen Square, social unrest in modern-day China has been rare. But the risk of popular unrest is going up as a result of widening income inequality, slowing—although still intense—economic growth, and continuing official abuse and corruption. The urban unemployed and migrant workers could stage protests; rural rebellion over land reclamations and onerous administrative fees could escalate. China's leaders might then clamp down on the media, religious groups, use of the Internet, and other forms of expression and communication. Faced with international criticism, the government could become more antagonistic and dogmatic about issues of concern to the United States and East Asia.

The probability of such events occurring in the short-term is low, but China's risk indicators suggest it is rising.

system will follow its economic trend line or vice versa is a fascinating and hotly contested subject in the political analyst community. (See the sidebar "Why China Keeps Us Up at Night.")

Corporate executives, however, generally focus on more immediate concerns when assessing a country's ripeness for investment. Broadly speaking, decision makers must know three things: How likely is it that a shock will occur? If likely, when will it probably occur? And how high are the stakes if it does?

The greatest risk, not surprisingly, is when shocks are likely, imminent, and have widespread consequences.

All three conditions exist in North Korea, which has remained stable only by resisting movement toward market economics and more open government. North Korea's stability is so dependent on Kim Jong Il and the country's military elite that any threat to their safety could destroy the regime and destabilize the entire region very quickly. And the stakes are high because the most valuable products North Korea has to sell—military and nuclear components—tend to produce political shocks.

In other nations, shocks are likely and expected to occur relatively soon, but the stakes for world markets are much lower. Fidel Castro, for example, is 78, and the fate of the revolution after his death is unclear. Castro's hard-line younger brother Raul might assume power, but he is also in his 70s; if he replaces Castro, political uncertainty will build until the next transfer of power. Similarly, if a reformer like Carlos Lage steps forward to begin a process of gradual opening, the release of long-repressed dissent could spark violence. So either outcome will probably produce instability. But because Cuba is not an exporter of nuclear technology, oil, or any other vital resource, the shock's effect on world markets will be minor.

Risk by the Numbers

Speculation on the outcomes of these and other scenarios appears in numerous publications, but corporations debating operational or infrastructure investments abroad need more objective, rigorous assessments than those found in the op-ed pages. Companies can either buy political risk services from consultants or, like Shell and AIG, develop the capacity in-house. Either way, a complete and accurate picture of any country's risk requires analysts with strong reportorial skills; timely, accurate data on a variety of social and political trends; and a framework for evaluating the impact of individual risks on stability.

The Analysts

Politics never stops moving, and risk analysts must be able to follow a nation's story as it develops. Usually, that means being on the ground in that country. And in the case of a particularly opaque regime, it can mean being there a very long time. Some information is published in official reports or in the media, but analysts will gather most of their intelligence from primary sources: well-connected journalists in the local and foreign press, current and former midlevel officials, and think tank specialists.

Companies should bear in mind that political analysis is more subjective and consequently more vulnerable to bias than its economic counterpart. One danger is that analysts with their own political opinions may view their research through a particular philosophical scrim. In addition, political analysts will probably have subject-matter—as well as nation-specific—expertise that can color their reports. A Taiwan analyst with a background in security, for example, may overemphasize such risk variables as cross-strait tensions and the growing imbalance of military power between Taiwan and China. An Eastern Europe analyst studying social unrest may insist that demonstrations by pensioners have the largest political impact on the government. As decision makers peruse analysts' reports, they should be alert for any potential bias and correct for it.

The Data

Because of their very nature, political risk variables are more difficult to measure than economic variables (although in some countries, such as China and Saudi Arabia, even the reliability of government-produced economic data is open to question). Politics, after all, is influenced by human behavior and the sudden confluence of events, for which no direct calibrations exist. How do you assign numbers to such concepts as the rule of law?

To accurately quantify political risk, then, analysts need proxies for their variables. Instead of trying to measure the independence of a nation's judiciary, for example, analysts can determine whether judges in a particular country are paid a living wage, whether funded programs exist to inform them about new legislation, and whether—and how often—they are targeted for assassination. Political risk analysts also study the percentage of children who regularly attend school, how police and military salaries compare with criminal opportunities, and how much access to medical care is available in towns with populations of 10,000 to 50,000 people. They look at such statistics as the unemployment rate for people between the ages of 18 and 29 and determine how many of them are in prison. And, of course, they add economic variables to the mix: per capita income, balance of payments, and national debt.

Taken together, this often anecdotal information reveals much about a country's underlying sources of strength or vulnerability. Comparing data from neighboring countries provides a good sense of where shocks from unstable nations might rumble into stable ones. Comparing a single nation's data points over time tells the analyst whether that nation is becoming more stable or less so, and how quickly.

The Framework

Different companies and consultancies will have different methods for measuring and presenting stability data. We at Eurasia Group have developed a tool that incorporates 20 composite indicators of risk in emerging markets. Distributed as part of a strategic relationship with Deutsche Bank, the Deutsche Bank Eurasia Group Stability Index (DESIX) scores risk variables according to both their structural and temporal components. Structural scores highlight long-term underlying conditions that affect stability. They then serve as a baseline for temporal scores, which reflect the impact of policies, events, and developments that occur each month.

The indicators are organized into four equally weighted subcategories: government, society, security, and the economy. Ratings for all four subcategories are aggregated into a single composite stability rating, which is expressed as a number on a scale of zero

Political risk at a glance

Political risk measures the stability of individual countries based on factors grounded in government, society, security, and the economy. Emerging markets are generally in the moderate- to high-stability range. The map shows how some countries scored in March 2005.

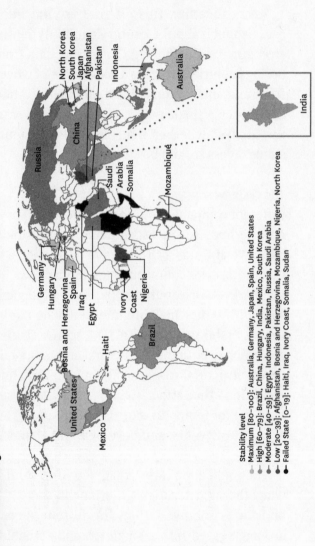

Stability level
- Maximum [80–100]: Australia, Germany, Japan, Spain, United States
- High [60–79]: Brazil, China, Hungary, India, Mexico, South Korea
- Moderate [40–59]: Egypt, Indonesia, Pakistan, Russia, Saudi Arabia
- Low [20–39]: Afghanistan, Bosnia and Herzegovina, Mozambique, Nigeria, North Korea
- Failed State [0–19]: Haiti, Iraq, Ivory Coast, Somalia, Sudan

Anatomy of India's political risk

National stability scores are plotted over time and comprise dozens of measurements, ranging from hard economic data on growth and investment to more amorphous assessments of youth disaffection and corruption. At the beginning of this year, India was hovering between moderate and high stability. (The numbers used to obtain each average have been rounded off.)

Factors affecting stability	Stability scores (0–100)			Comments
	Jan 2005	Feb 2005	Mar 2005	
Government (such as strength of current government, rule of law, and level of corruption)	67	64	62	Political missteps by the government led to poor performance in state elections and strengthened opposition parties.
Society (such as social tension, youth disaffection, and health, education, and other services)	58	58	58	Low per capita income and literacy levels lead to a low human development index. Simmering social tensions keep the society score low.
Security (such as level of globalization, geostrategic condition, and emergencies and disasters)	53	48	48	Peace talks with Pakistan and China have eased security fears. But a Maoist insurgency in Nepal and continuing Kashmir violence keep the score low.
Economy (such as fiscal condition, growth and investment, and external sector and debt)	75	75	76	Economic growth and expanding trade keep the numbers healthy. The fiscal deficit remains a worry.
Cumulative National Stability Score	63	61	62	

Source: Deutsche Bank Eurasia Group Stability Index (DESIX), March 2005

to 100—from a failed state to a fully institution-alized, stable democracy. (See the exhibits "Political Risk at a Glance" and "Anatomy of India's Political Risk.")

Very often, the numbers that make up the stability rating are as interesting as the stability rating itself. Consider Turkey, whose March 2005 stability rating was 60, five points lower than Brazil's and two points higher than Russia's. Within that composite number, components are moving in opposite directions.

Specifically, Turkey's government rating rose as a consequence of the European Union agreement to open accession talks with Ankara in October 2005. Prime Minister Recep Tayyip Erdogan's administration now has greater incentive to continue reforms that strengthen the independence of Turkey's institutions, increase media freedom, and protect the rights of minority groups—such as Turkish Kurds—who might otherwise provoke unrest. Turkish membership in the EU would also bind the country more closely to European institutions, further increasing stability.

Yet Turkey's security rating is pushed lower by the continued presence of Kurdistan Workers' Party militants in northern Iraq. Ankara worries that the Kurds—empowered by the Iraqi elections—may try to regain control of the oil-rich northern Iraqi town of Kirkuk, which would provide the financial basis for an independent Kurdish state. A Kurdish state on Turkey's borders would likely fan separatist flames in that country's own Kurdish population.

Once You Know the Odds

How companies apply such analysis obviously depends upon their industry, strategy, and risk tolerance profile. Of necessity, companies in the energy industry, for example, have demonstrated a high tolerance for risk, relying on mitigation techniques to manage their exposure. By contrast, light manufacturers and midsize companies in industrial supply chains tend to bide their time to see how situations evolve. And pharmaceutical corporations generally shy away from investment when presented with infrastructure or intellectual property risks.

Companies making extended commitments in unstable nations must give top priority to long-term risk—issues related to demographics and natural resources, for example—when making decisions. In May 2004, Japan's Sumitomo Chemical agreed to a $4.3 billion joint venture with Saudi Aramco to build a major petrochemical plant at Rabigh in Saudi Arabia. The plant isn't scheduled to open until 2008, so Sumitomo is particularly vulnerable to such pernicious demographic trends as the exodus of technical talent and the joblessness of young men.

Sumitomo's risk tolerance is already being tested by an Islamic extremist campaign of kidnapping and beheading foreigners who do business in the country. But while violence and corruption dominate headlines, such near-term risks are much exaggerated. (See the sidebar "Why Saudi Arabia Keeps Us Up at Night.")

Why Saudi Arabia Keeps Us Up at Night

SAUDI ARABIA'S STABILITY is under fire from religious and secular forces. Islamic extremists hope to undermine the legitimacy of the royal family. Real unemployment is estimated to be between 20% and 25%; frustrated, jobless young men are flocking to mosques and schools where religious leaders thunder against the infidels. Western nations, meanwhile, are calling on the royals to move toward political liberalization. And the flight of expatriates will eventually take its toll on the Saudis' ability to diversify their economy.

Such volatility complicates financial deals—particularly those that take years to assemble—and extends the exposure to political risk over time.

But while companies with long-term investments must worry, short-term investors in Saudi Arabia have less cause for concern. That's because oil money stabilizes the political system, and the royal family can count on those revenues for years to come. Yes, oil supplies are a tempting target for terrorists; but the country's oil infrastructure is isolated from population centers, and redundancies in the pipeline system make it almost impossible to inflict lasting damage with a single blow. In addition, the national oil company has the technology, the trained engineers, and the spare capacity to continue producing significantly more than 9 million barrels per day. Finally, in light of concerns that foreign governments might freeze Saudi assets following September 11, 2001, a great deal of money flowed back into the kingdom, providing the House of Saud with more ready cash.

Clearly, any project in Saudi Arabia that needs a decade to show a profit is deeply problematic. But those willing to brave volatility in the near term may profit from opportunities that more risk-averse companies forgo.

In fact, although Saudi Arabia—and China, too—may be risky bets for companies engaged in ventures that won't see profitability for a decade, in the short run there is money to be made. Among others, General Motors, Kodak, and a number of investment banks have already done so—though they've stumbled a bit in the process.

Once companies have determined that a particular investment is worth the danger, they can use traditional techniques to mitigate the risk—recruiting local partners, for example, or limiting R&D in nations with leaky intellectual property protection. In addition, a growing number of commercial and government organizations now offer insurance against political risks such as the expropriation of property, political violence, currency inconvertibility, and breach of contract. (Such insurance is expensive, however, because risks are so hard to assess.) Otherwise it's mostly a matter of hedging—locating a factory in Mexico as well as Venezuela, say, so as not to bet the entire Latin America strategy on a single opaque regime.

Finally, it is worth remembering that though instability translates into greater risk, risk is not always a bad thing. Political risk in underdeveloped countries nearly always carries an upside because such nations are so unstable that negative shocks can do little further damage. On the stability ladder, for example, Afghanistan and Cambodia simply don't have far to fall; only favorable external conditions—such as debt relief from the developed world or loans from international institutions—could have much effect on their political stability. For some companies, that could make investments in such countries an attractive part of an enterprise risk portfolio.

Politics has always been inseparable from markets; the world's first transnational trade organizations were moved by the political waves of their time. Today, goods, services, information, ideas, and people cross borders with unprecedented velocity—and the trend is only intensifying. For company leaders seeking profit in places that are socially, culturally, and governmentally alien, the complementary insights of political and economic risk analysts are vital.

IAN BREMMER is the president of Eurasia Group, a political-risk consulting firm, and a senior fellow at the World Policy Institute in New York.

Originally published in June 2005. Reprint R0506B

Index

You don't want to miss these...

We've combed through hundreds of *Harvard Business Review* articles on key management topics and selected *the* most important ones to help you maximize your own and your organization's performance.